Beyond Space

By

Rev. Pascal P. Parente, S.T.D., Ph.D., J.C.B.

TAN BOOKS AND PUBLISHERS, INC.
Rockford, Illinois 61105

NIHIL OBSTAT:
  Joseph D. Brokhage, S.T.D.
  Censor Librorum

IMPRIMATUR:
  Paul C. Schulte, D.D.
  Archbishop of Indianapolis
  December 28, 1957

Originally published by the Society of St. Paul.

ISBN: 0-89555-053-9

Printed and bound in the United States of America.

TAN BOOKS AND PUBLISHERS, INC.
P.O. Box 424
Rockford, Illinois 61105

1973

PUBLISHER'S PREFACE

We are returning *Beyond Space* to print because people want to know about the angels and because Father Parente's book goes a long way toward teaching us about them. Granted, this is a brief and somewhat popularly written treatise; it is withal a scholarly one and can well serve to pique our thoughts and stimulate our researches toward further understanding.

Men, however civilized and citified and spirtually dulled they may be from the incessant "noise" of modern society, are still possessed of intellect, and in fact discern within the incohate reaches of their minds that man and the material world do not exhaust the possibilities of God's creation and that perhaps "beyond space," to use the author's expression, there exists an entire realm of heavenly beings. And this very real possibility enthralls the mind of man, making a study of the angels of profound interest.

We of the Faith, of course, take the existence of angels for granted, but how much do we really know about them? The author has here come to instruct us with a broad sketch of the Church's teaching on the subject. May it serve to enlighten and inspire its readers and instill in them a deeper love for and devotion to the angels, as well as increase their love and respect for our holy Catholic Faith.

Thomas A. Nelson
January 8, 1973

About the Author

Dr. Pascal P. Parente, Ph.D., S.T.D., J.C.B., scholar, professor, and author, had a long-standing reputation as the foremost authority on ascetical and mystical theology in the United States. For twenty-two years he was professor of these subjects at Catholic University of America, and for three years Dean of the School of Sacred Theology.

The secret of Father Parente's great popularity as a professor and author lay in his ability to express profound thought in simple, every-day language. In addition to numerous articles in theological magazines, Encyclopedia Brittannica, and the Catholic Encyclopedia, Father Parente published the following books: *The Ascetical Life, The Mystical Life, The Well of Living Waters, Susanna Mary Beardsworth, The Case of Padre Pio, School Teacher and Saint, and Beyond Space.*

In June, 1960, Father Parente retired to his country home in Cambridge, New York, where he divided his time between scholarly pursuits and gardening, his favorite hobby. He expressed the hope that, at last, he would have the opportunity to write the many books for which "the busy life of a professor left no time."

In 1970 the author passed to his eternal reward.

CONTENTS

Part I

THE SPIRIT WORLD

Part II

Our Guardian Angels and Angelophanies

PART I

THE SPIRIT WORLD

Chapter I

THE ANGELS

Morning Stars of Creation

PURE spirits, the closest image and likeness of the Creator, were the effect of a divine act of creation. A spirit world was produced, at once, in its fullness and in its grandeur. When, at the word of the Almighty, light's first rays lit up the primeval, shapeless world, still "wrapped in a mist as in swaddling clothes," a wondrous song, a joyful melody filled the new heavens with never-ending strains. The Lord recalls these primordial times when He asks: "Where wast thou when I laid the foundations of the earth? . . . When the morning stars praised me together, and all the sons of God made joyful melody."[1] These "sons of God," living witnesses of the creation of the material universe, were our Angels, the morning stars of creation.

It is an article of faith, firmly established in Scripture and Tradition, and clearly expressed in Christian Doctrine from the beginning, that this spirit world, our Angels, began with time and was created by God. This traditional belief of both the Old and the New Testament was given a more formal and solemn expression in the fourth Lateran Council in 1215: (God)

---

[1] Job 38:4, 7. As a matter of fact, the Greek version of the Septuagint of the book of Job, which is a rendition of the accepted sense rather than of the letter of the text, translates "sons of God" of our Vulgate as "Angels," and the same verse reads as follows: "When the stars were made, all my angels praised me with a great voice."

"by his almighty power created together in the beginning of time both creatures, the spiritual and the corporeal, namely the Angelic and the earthly, and afterwards the human, as it were an intermediate creature, composed of body and spirit."[2]

From this definition we learn that the Angelic spirits were created when time began and not from eternity. Like all other creatures they were produced by the almighty power of God, out of nothing. It would be heretical to affirm that the Angels are an emanation of the divine substance.[3] Spiritual substances do not divide or split or multiply in any form whatever, nor change one into another; their individual existence can only be explained by creation.

The creation of the Angels is implicitly affirmed in all those passages of Sacred Scripture in which it is stated that all things were made by God; explicitly and formally their creation is mentioned by Saint Paul in one of those incomplete enumerations of the Angelic orders: "In Him (the Son of God, the Logos) were all things created in heaven and on earth, visible and invisible, whether Thrones, or Dominations, or Principalities, or Powers: all things were created by Him and in Him."[4]

Creation itself is a revealed truth, not so the exact time when the Angels were created. Nothing definite can be determined on this point from Sacred Scripture. Neither Jewish nor Christian Tradition agrees on the time when the spirit world, our Angels, came into existence. With many of the Fathers of the Church we believe as very probable that the Angels were created long before the material world. They were certainly created before man, because we find them already distinguished as good Angels and fallen angels on man's first appearance on earth.[5]

---

[2] D. 428. A similar definition was given in the Vatican Council in 1869, D. 1782, 1801.

[3] Vatican Council, D. 1804.

[4] Col. 1:16.

[5] Gen. 3:1 ff.; 3:24.

This circumstance would seem to imply that a long time, one or more cosmic period, had elapsed from the time of their creation. It does not seem probable that God, Who created this world for His own glory, would have no created intelligences to witness the awe-inspiring act of its making. The passage from Job quoted above seems to prove that such witnesses did exist. They saw the marvelous manifestations of the Divine Wisdom, Power, and Goodness and praised the Lord, filling the heavens with "joyful melody." Man himself was not there at the beginning of creation to give glory to God; some created intelligence must have been present. The Angels were the first splendors created to reflect the glory of the Eternal. The first creative act must have produced a creature to the image and similitude of God, a creature able to understand, love, thank, and praise God. When the whole material world had been created, the Lord formed another similar creature, "a little less than the Angels," consisting of body and spirit, able to know, love, and serve Him on earth as the Angels do in heaven. We like to imagine the creation of the material universe placed between the creations of two orders of rational beings. One, heavenly, purely spiritual: the Angels; one, earthly, partly material, partly spiritual: Man.[6]

Saint Thomas, with some of the Fathers of the Church, regards as more probable the opinion maintaining that the Angels

[6] This opinion is thus expressed in the *Constitutions of the Apostles,* in the Liturgy of the Mass, called *Clementina:* "By Him (Thy only begotten Son) didst Thou make, before all things, the Cherubim and the Seraphim, the Aeons and the Hosts, the Powers and Authorities, Principalities and Thrones, the Archangels and Angels. And after all these, didst Thou make the visible world by Him, and all the things that are therein." And in St. Ambrose: "Even though the Angels, the Dominations and the Powers had a beginning, they were already there when this world was made." *Hexaemeron,* I, 5, 19. The same opinion is defended by St. Jerome *(Super Epist. ad Titum, I),* St. John Damascene *(De Fide Orthodoxa, III, 3),* and others.

were created together with the material universe because they are part of that universe. He does not regard as erroneous the opinion of those who hold that they were created before the visible world.[7] The peculiar astronomical notions common in his day attributed to the Angels many duties that pertained to the physical government of the world, and thus they appeared more as a necessary part of the visible world than they actually are.

Another reason for that opinion is the authority of some of the Fathers who saw the creation of the Angels in the words of Genesis, chapter 1:1, more exactly in the creation of heaven: "In the beginning God created heaven and earth." Thus, for example, Saint Epiphanius: "The word of God clearly declares that the Angels were neither created after the stars nor before heaven and earth. It must be regarded as certain and unshakable the opinion that says: None of the created things did exist before heaven and earth, because 'in the beginning God created heaven and earth' so that this was the beginning of all creation, before which none of the created things existed."[8] Origen, however, is more careful with his opinion: "This also is part of the doctrine of the Church, that there are certain Angels of God and certain good Powers, which are His servants in accomplishing the salvation of men. When these, however, were created, or of what nature they are, or how they exist, is not clearly stated."[9] He does not read in the words of Genesis what is not written there. Modern Scripture scholars reject as unfounded the opinion of those who see the creation of the Angels in the creation of heaven. Thus, according to Ceuppens, the whole account of Genesis, chapter 1:1, treats only of things visible, not of the invisible and immaterial: "Heaven and earth

[7] *Summa Theologica*, Pars I, Q. 61, art. 3.
[8] *Adversus Haereses*, Panar., 65, 5.
[9] *De Principiis*, Preface, 10.

is an expression used by the Hebrews to mean the whole visible universe, the cosmos, the well-ordered world as we see it."[10] Even more emphatic is Father Von Hummelauer: "Now the Angels are certainly not meant by the word *heaven*, because they are never called *heaven* ... nor does the context offer sufficient reason for us to affirm that Angels are truly implied even though only implicitly."[11]

The wording of the definition by the Lateran Council, reported before, which seems to be opposed to the opinion of priority of creation of the Angels, creates no difficulty whatever. It is said there that God "created together *(simul)* in the beginning of time both creatures, the spiritual and the corporeal, namely the Angelic and the earthly." It is commonly admitted that the word "together" *(simul)* in this case has not the meaning of parity of time or simultaneousness, but parity of action. The expression was taken from Scripture where it is said: "He that liveth forever created all things together,"[12] meaning not that all things were created at the same time, but that all things were likewise created with no indication of time. Saint Thomas points out that this definition of the Lateran Council was aimed at a Manichaean heresy of emanation. It did not bear on the time of creation of the Angels but on the fact that they were produced by the act of creation, just like the corporeal, earthly creatures.[13]

Both the existence and the creation of the Angels are dogmas of faith presenting one of the most inspiring and consoling aspects of our Religion. As the first creatures of this universe, the Angels were the first revelation of the Supreme Goodness of God and of His transcendent Beauty. Even though part of the universe, the Angels really constitute a world to themselves, the

---

[10] F. Ceuppens, *De Historia Primaeva*, p. 9.
[11] *Commentarius in Genesim*, p. 88.
[12] Ecclus. 18:1.
[13] *Opusculum* XXIII.

spirit world, so exalted and so different from our visible, material world.

When God created the first life in this world He bade it to multiply upon the earth. The Lord blessed the first human couple He had created, saying: "Increase and multiply and fill the earth."[14] It took mankind many thousands of years to discover and fill most of the earth. Not so with the spirit world. There are no more Angels today than when they were first created at the beginning of time. They filled the heavens from the start, and their number was complete from the beginning. Their spiritual nature, just like our human soul, cannot be produced except by the Divine act of creation, with the difference that the human soul is created only in the course of time, when it is needed to inform a human body at the time of generation. Except for the apostasy and desertion of the fallen angels, the Angelic family has remained the same from the time it was called into being by the loving Father of all.

No matter when the Angels began, there was a time in that endless eternity when the Angels, like all the other creatures, did not exist. The Eternal Wisdom, the Word of God, refers to such an epoch in the timeless existence of God, where It says: "The Lord possessed me in the beginning of His ways, before He made anything from the beginning."[15] Therefore, they were not created from all eternity but in the beginning of time.

The Population of the Angelic World

The exact number of Angels that inhabit the heavenly Jerusalem has not been revealed. To try to determine their number must appear like an idle question, since man has not been able even to determine the exact number of stars. The vast number of

[14] Gen. 1:28.
[15] Prov. 8:22.

stars, each one a sun in itself, is awe-inspiring and quite beyond our powers of comprehension. Until now, no known mechanical device has been able to even remotely suggest the magnitude of this visible universe. What must be the magnitude, the splendor, and glory of the invisible, immutable Angelic part of the universe? What the vastness of the spirit world, the number of those splendors that decorate the heavenly home, the House of God, if the house of man, our earth, is surrounded by such an infinity of stars? Who has ever been able to count all the men and women who have inhabited this earth from the beginning to the present time?

Without Divine revelation we would be unable to know not only the number of Angels but even whether they exist at all. It is then on the data of revelation that we must depend in order to give some vague idea of the transcending vastness of the spirit world. These data actually suggest a multitude of Angels that is beyond all our power of comprehension.

Describing the throne of God surrounded by heavenly spirits, the prophet Daniel is at a loss in determining the number of those heavenly beings, our good Angels: "Thousands of thousands ministered to Him, and ten thousand times a hundred thousand stood before Him."[16] Bible commentators tell us that the figures here given by Daniel do not express a definite number. They serve to convey the idea of a multitude that is far beyond the power of human language to express. More than figures, they are really hyperbolical expressions for an innumerable multitude of Angels standing around the throne of God.[17]

The throne of the Most High, surrounded by His hosts of myriads and myriads of Angels, is a picture occurring frequently

[16] 7:10.
[17] J. Knabenbauer, *Commentarius in Danielem Prophetam*, p. 195. *See also* R. V. O'Connell, *The Holy Angels*, p. 105; and C. F. Keil, *The Book of the Prophet Daniel*, p. 230.

in the Scriptures of the Old Testament. "I saw the Lord sitting on His throne, and all the army of heaven standing by Him on the right hand and on the left."[18] Awe-inspiring is the vision described by the Prophet Isaias: "I saw the Lord sitting upon a throne high and elevated, and his train filled the temple. Upon it stood the Seraphims, the one had six wings, and the other had six wings: with two they covered his face, and with two they covered his feet, and with two they flew. And they cried one to another, and said: Holy, holy, holy, the Lord God of hosts, all the earth is full of his glory."[19] Saint John the Evangelist, in his Apocalypse, describes a vision of many thousands of Angels round about the throne of God: "And I beheld, and I heard the voice of many Angels round about the throne . . . and the number of them was thousands of thousands."[20]

Saint Thomas holds that the multitude of the Angels far exceeds every multitude of material creatures,[21] quoting to this effect from Pseudo Dionysius who wrote: "The scriptural tradition regarding the Angels gives their number as thousands of thousands, multiplying and repeating the very highest numbers we have, thus clearly showing that the Orders of the Celestial Beings are innumerable for us. So many are the blessed Hosts of the Supernal Intelligences that they wholly surpass the feeble and limited range of our material numbers."[22] The more perfect creatures, writes Saint Thomas in the same article of the *Summa*, are produced in greater number, because God intends primarily the perfection of the universe in the production of things. With this principle in mind it is easy to understand how the number of the Angelic spirits must exceed beyond all comparison the number of human souls created from the be-

[18] III Kings 22:19.
[19] Isa. 6:1 ff.
[20] 5:11.
[21] *Summa Theo.*, I, Q. 50, art. 3.
[22] *De Caelesti Hierarchia*, XIV.

ginning of the world until now and to be created from now to the end of the world.

When we speak of the number of Angels we refer to the good Angels who now live with God and minister to Him both in Heaven and on earth, that portion of the spirit world which remained faithful to God after the fall of Lucifer and his rebellious spirits.

Nothing is revealed about the number of the fallen angels. However, some theologians believe to have found something like a proportion between good Angels and demons (fallen angels) in the words of the Apocalypse: "Behold a great red dragon, having seven heads and ten horns, and on his head seven diadems; and his tail drew the third part of the stars of heaven, and cast them to the earth."[23] The stars of heaven are understood by these authors to be a figure of speech for Angels and the red dragon for Satan. "On the strength of this text certain mystically inclined theologians estimate the proportion of the fallen angels to those that remained faithful as one to three, 1:3. Whether this estimate be correct or no, we may safely assume that the number of the faithful Angels exceeded those who fell away."[24]

An event that took place in the days of the prophet Eliseus seems to corroborate the view that there are many more of the good Angels than of the fallen ones; many more on our side than against us. A vast army of Syrians had been sent to apprehend the prophet who was alone with his servant. At the sight of the Syrian army, the servant became deadly frightened not knowing that a more powerful Angelic army had been sent invisibly by God to defend the prophet: "And the servant of the man of God [Eliseus] rising early, went out, and saw an

[23] Apoc. 12:3 f.
[24] Pohle-Preuss, *God the Author of Nature and the Supernatural*, p. 341.

army round about the city, and horses and chariots; and he told him saying: Alas, alas, alas, my lord, what shall we do? But he answered: Fear not, for there are more with us than with them. And Eliseus prayed and said: Lord, open his eyes that he may see. And the Lord opened the eyes of the servant, and he saw, and behold the mountain was full of horses and chariots of fire round about Eliseus."[25]

This powerful array of the heavenly armies ready to defend one of God's prophets reminds us of the Divine Savior Who, at the very moment of being delivered into the hands of His enemies, reminded the over-zealous Simon Peter, "Thinkest thou that I cannot ask my Father, and he will give me presently more than twelve legions of Angels?"[26]

What interests us, at present, are those "twelve legions of Angels." A legion of soldiers, in New Testament times, was composed ordinarily of 6,826 men. Perhaps we should not take the expression as a definite number but rather as a symbolic figure of a vast multitude. In that dark and sad hour that marked the beginning of His great humiliation, the Savior calls God His Father and reminds His disciples that the hosts of heaven are at His command. One of those heavenly spirits had come down to comfort Him.[27] Far more numerous than all the stars of heaven, all the flowers of spring, and all the children of men are God's Angels, the blessed citizens of the spirit world, the fulgid, glittering morning stars of creation.

What is an Angel?

"The Angels are spirits," says Saint Augustine, "but it is not because they are spirits that they are Angels. They become Angels when they are sent, for the name Angel refers to their

[25] IV Kings 6:15 ff.
[26] Matt. 26:53.
[27] Luke 22:43.

office not to their nature. You ask the name of this nature, it is *spirit;* you ask its office, it is that of an Angel, (i.e., a messenger). In as far as he exists, an Angel is a spirit; in as far as he acts, he is an Angel."[28] The word "angel," comes from a Greek word meaning "messenger." In the Scriptures of the Old Testament, the most frequently used name to designate the Angels is *mal'akh,* which means, messenger or legate.

This generic name "angel" does not reveal anything about the real nature of those celestial beings besides the fact that they are occasionally sent on a mission as messengers or legates of God to men. Because only on such occasions, and in such a quality, they make themselves visible to men, they have been given the name of messengers from the most common duty and office they fulfill towards God's children here on earth. "And to the Angels indeed he saith: 'He that maketh his Angels spirits, and his ministers a flame of fire.' "[29]

The office of being a messenger, an angel, is neither the most important nor the most common among the duties of the celestial spirits in the court of Heaven; it alone does not offer enough ground for speculation on their true nature and operation.

Heaven is the true country of the good Angels: "Their Angels [of the little ones] in heaven always see the face of my Father who is in heaven."[30] Even while engaged here on earth as guardians of the little children, they remain the blessed comprehensors, enjoying the vision of God, "the face of my Father." They are by grace the happy citizens of the heavenly Jerusalem from the beginning.

[28] *Serm. in Ps. 103,* I, 15.

[29] Hebr. 1:7. In this passage Saint Paul quotes verse 4 of Psalm 103, the same verse Saint Augustine commented on in the above quotation. Literally that verse should read: "Who makest thy messengers the winds, and thy ministers the burning fire." Saint Paul, and with him Saint Augustine and many other Fathers, interpret that verse allegorically and apply it to the heavenly messengers of God, the Angels.

[30] Matt. 18:10.

"Let us remember," writes Saint Bernard, "that the citizens of that country are spirits, mighty, glorious, blessed, distinct personalities, of graduated rank, occupying the order given them from the beginning, perfect of their kind ... endowed with immortality, passionless, not so created, but so made—that is, through grace, not by nature; being of pure mind, benignant affections, religious and devout; of unblemished morality; inseparably one in heart and mind, blessed with unbroken peace, God's edifice dedicated to the divine praises and service. All this we ascertain by reading, and hold by faith."[31]

All this is really what we gather and ascertain by reading the sources, Scripture and Tradition, regarding the nature, character, and blessed condition of the Angels. All the qualities of the Angelic spirits listed here by Saint Bernard are most beautiful and they are theologically correct. However, we have omitted one of the qualifications from the above passage in order to make the quotation perfect. The words omitted are these: "having ethereal bodies." On this very important point of the perfect spirituality of the Angelic nature there still remained some confusion in the days of Saint Bernard, as it had been the case for several centuries during the Patristic period. Saint Bernard expresses his doubts and hesitation on this point when he adds: "As regards their (the Angels') bodies some authorities hesitate to say not only whence they are derived, but whether in any real sense they (the bodies) exist at all. If anyone is inclined to think the derivation of these bodies a matter of opinion, I do not dispute the point."[32] It is Catholic doctrine[33] today, even though not yet an article of faith, that the Angels are pure spirits, incorporeal substances, free and independent from any material body, ethereal or otherwise.

[31] *De Consideratione*, Lib. V, cap. 4.
[32] *Ibid.*
[33] D. 428, 1783.

By "pure spirit" we understand a subsistent intelligent being whose subtle and transcendent nature is in no wise whatever composed of matter, however refined and ethereal. An Angel then is such a spirit. Both his existence and operation are free and independent from matter; nor is the Angel related to a body, like the human soul, which even though perfectly spiritual, is naturally related to the human body as an essential part of the whole human nature. The Angelic nature is wholly spiritual, man's nature is composed of body and spirit.

One of the reasons why so many of the ancient writers, including a good many among the Fathers, attributed subtle bodies to the Angels, even while admitting their spiritual nature, is the fact that for them the words "body" and "spirit" did not have that definite and perfect philosophical meaning which those words acquired especially during the Scholastic period of Christian philosophy. Such a cloudy philosophical notion, for example, appears manifest in the *Catecheses* of Saint Cyril of Jerusalem. For him, whatever has not a gross body can rightly be called a spirit; so that the air we breathe, any vapor or gaseous matter was called spirit or spiritual body.[34] They attributed such kind of bodies to Angels. Others made a distinction between earthly bodies and heavenly bodies, attributing a subtle, rarefied nature to the latter. They were confirmed, it seems, in this erroneous opinion by a false interpretation of Genesis, chapter 6:2 ff., according to which the "sons of God" mentioned there, who took to themselves wives and procreated children, were erroneously understood by them to be Angels; whereas they were human beings, the descendants of the religious and devout Seth and Henos. Then again, they were led to believe that those ethereal human forms assumed by the Angels in their various apparitions here on earth were part of their Angelic nature. Saint Basil the Great believed that the Angelic

[34] *Catecheses,* XVI, 15.

nature was a "breath of air or an immaterial fire."[35] This is why they are localized, he said, and become visible, in the form and shape of their own bodies, to those who are worthy to see them. We find these notions about ethereal bodies both among the Greek and the Latin Fathers. While Saint Jerome has nothing definite regarding the nature of the Angels, he rejects the argument in favor of a corporeal nature inferred from Genesis. Saint Augustine thought it more probable that they had subtle bodies. According to him the demons, before their fall, had such heavenly bodies; since their fall, however, their bodies consist of damp, thick air.[36] Cassian clearly expresses the same opinion in these words: "Even though we define as spiritual some of the substances, such as the Angels, the Archangels, and the other powers, as also our own souls and certainly this subtle air, nevertheless they are by no means to be regarded as incorporeal, for in their own way they possess a body whereby they subsist, even though it is a much more subtle one than our own. . . . Hence it appears that God alone is incorporeal."[37] It is more surprising to find the same opinion expressed by Saint John Damascene, who knew the writings of Pseudo Dionysius on this subject for which he had great admiration. While expressing some hesitation regarding the true nature of an Angel and while defining him as *asomatos* (without a body) he finally agrees with the current philosophy of calling the angelic nature "gross and material" if compared to God. "An Angel is an intellectual substance, endowed with liberty, perpetually active, without a body, serving God, having attained immortality by a gift of grace, the form and the limits of whose substance only its Creator knows. However, it is said to be incorporeal and immaterial only in reference to us, for anything compared to God,

---

[35] *De Spiritu Sancto,* 38.
[36] *De Genes. ad Litt.,* III, 14, 15; *De Civ. Dei,* XXI, 10, etc.
[37] *Collationes,* VII, 13.

Who alone is incomparable, is found to be gross and material. The divine nature alone is immaterial and incorporeal."[38] In the West, Saint Gregory the Great, while not completely free of the philosophy of "spiritual bodies," inclines vigorously towards the opinion of Pseudo Dionysius that makes the Angels pure spiritual beings.[39]

Discussing the term "incorporeal" Origen writes: "The term 'incorporeal' is disused and unknown, not only in many other writings but also in our own Scriptures." He then explains the expression "an incorporeal demon" by saying: "It must be understood that he [Christ] had not such a body as demons have, which is naturally fine and thin, as if formed of air (and for this reason is either considered or called by many incorporeal), but that he [Christ] had a solid and palpable body. Now, according to human custom, everything which is not of that nature is called by the simple and ignorant incorporeal; as if one were to say that the air which we breathe was incorporeal."[40]

From what has been said so far we must conclude that the terms "spirit" and "spiritual" were not taken by all in the same sense in which they are taken and understood today, in reference to the Angelic nature. A number of the earlier Scholastics retained the view of ethereal bodies in the case of the Angels, as Rupert of Deutz, Saint Bernard (as we have seen), and Peter Lombard. On the other hand Robert Pulleyn and Hugh of Saint Victor contended that the Angels must be regarded as pure spirits and immaterial beings. Owing to the position taken by the IV Lateran Council, the latter view became more common during the first part of of the thirteenth century. Even though the doctrine had not been defined by the Council, it had nevertheless been made quite clear to what class of creatures the Angels

---

[38] *De Fide Orthodoxa*, 2, 3.
[39] *Moral.*, II, 8; IV, 8; *Dialog.*, IV, 29.
[40] Origen, *De Principiis*, Preface, 8.

belong. The Council divided all creatures into three classes: the purely spiritual, the Angels; the purely material, the material world; and the partly spirit, partly matter, human beings. By one of his subtle theories, Scotus is said to have ascribed bodies to Angels but in an entirely different sense.[41] Saint Thomas with Saint Albertus Magnus, Henry of Ghent, Durandus and many others were in favor of the spirituality of the Angels in the strict sense of the word.[42]

This opinion of the Angelic Doctor regarding the nature of the Angels has become the common doctrine. They are pure spirits, not composed of matter and form, but composed of essence and existence, of act and potentiality. This doctrine is found already in the writings of Pseudo Dionysius[43] and of a

[41] *De Rerum Principiis,* Q. 7, art. 1, 2, 3. Some regard this opinion as wrongly attributed to Scotus by some Franciscan scholars. Rather than an ethereal body, he assigns to both Angels and human souls a *materia primo prima,* which is simply a passive potentiality *(potentia passiva)* material in its nature. He also attributes to both Angels and human souls a composition of matter and form, but because, he says, neither Angels nor human souls have a *forma corporeitatis* to complete the *materia primo prima,* they remain incorporeal, even though composed of matter and form.

[42] *Summa Theo.,* I, Q. 50, art. 2. All these writers did not admit the distinction of *materia primo prima* excogitated by Scotus, and attributed by them to all creatures alike. The Thomist principle was that material substances, and material substances alone, are composed of matter and form: "In material things there is one element which determines to a special grade, and that is form; and another element which is determined, and this is matter: . . . whereas in immaterial things there is no separate determinator and thing determined; each thing by its own self holds a determinate grade of being." Although there is no composition of matter and form in an Angel, yet there is act and potentiality. . . . Such a kind of composition is understood to be in the Angels; and this is what some say, that an Angel is composed of that whereby he is and that which is, or essence and existence, as Boethius says.

[43] *De Divinis Nominibus,* IV. "Through these (the rays of God's undivided goodness) all spiritual beings and virtues and powers (whether perceived or percipient) had their beginning. Through these they exist

few of the Fathers, whom Saint Thomas follows closely in this question.

In his work on *The Celestial Hierarchies,* Pseudo Dionysius thus describes the Godlike immateriality of the Angels and their superiority of nature above all other creatures: "Those natures which are around the Godhead (the Angels) have participated of It in many different ways. On this account the holy orders of the celestial beings are present with and participate in the Divine Principle in a degree far surpassing all those things which merely exist, all the irrational living beings, and rational human beings. For molding themselves intelligibly to the imitation of God, and looking in a supernal way to the Likeness of the Supreme Deity, and longing to form the intellectual image of it, they naturally have a more abundant communion with Him, and with unremitting activity they tend eternally up the steep, as far as is permitted, through the ardor of their unwearying divine love, and they receive the primal radiance in a pure and immaterial manner, adapting themselves to this in a life that is wholly intellectual."[44]

Because of their wholly spiritual and immaterial nature, the Angels occupy the first and highest place in the scale of created things. Man himself is second on the scale of creatures: "Thou hast made him [man] a little less than the Angels."[45] Just like an Angel because of his spiritual, immaterial soul, less than an Angel because of his material body.

and possess a life incapable of failure or diminution, and are untainted by any corruption or death or materiality or birth, being separate above all instability and flux and restlessness and change. And whereas they are bodiless and immaterial, they are perceived by our minds, and whereas they are minds themselves, they possess a supernatural perception and receive an illumination (after their own manner) concerning the hidden nature of things, from whence they pass on their own knowledge to other kindred spirits."

[44] *De Caelesti Hierarchia,* IV.
[45] Ps. 8:6.

Every Angel is a distinct being, an individual subsisting in an intellectual nature; consequently every Angel is a person. The classical definition of a person, by Boethius, applies to them most perfectly: A person is an individual substance of a rational nature. Every Angel is an individuated nature, endowed with intelligence and liberty, placed outside of its cause in the world of reality. All the essential elements of an individual personality are clearly manifest in those manifold accounts of Angels appearing in this world and dealing with man, as reported in the Bible, for example, the Archangel Raphael and young Tobias; Gabriel and the Virgin Mary; Gabriel and Saint Zachary. Rightly, therefore, Pope Pius XII condemns the opinion of those who "question whether Angels are personal beings."[46]

Not only are the Angels real personal beings but because of their spiritual nature wholly untrammeled by matter, their personality is far superior to human personality. Human beings differ from each other merely as individuals of the same species; Angels on the contrary, according to Saint Thomas, differ from each other specifically;[47] so that we may say that there are not two Angels of the same species; each of them is his own kind. This fact implies a far more perfect individuality, a higher form of personality than the one known to us. Because of this specific difference, it follows that every single Angelic creature reveals an entirely new aspect of the eternal beauty and glory of God. To them apply the words of Saint Paul: "Star differeth from star in glory."[48]

This is the wondrous Angelic world that the Lord created at the beginning of time. In our earthly way of thinking we may conceive it as a living diamond whose myriads of facets reflect constantly and harmoniously the divine splendors of the eternal

---

[46] Encyclical *Humani Generis*, 26.
[47] *Summa Theo.*, I, Q. 50, art. 4.
[48] I Cor. 15:41.

glory of God. Among all created things the Angels are the best reflectors of the divine light: "As our sun, through no choice or deliberation, but by the very fact of its existence, gives light to all those things which have any inherent power of sharing its illumination, even so the [supreme] Good ... sends forth upon all things according to their receptive powers, the rays of its undivided Goodness."[49]

[49] P. Dionysius, *De Div. Nom.*, IV.

Chapter II

THE ANGELIC NATURE AND ITS OPERATION

The Angelic Mind and Mode of Expression

AS pure spirits the Angels are created intelligences, altogether above matter and free from any essential relation to it, both in their existence and their operation. In this respect the Angels are specifically above the human soul which, even though of a spiritual nature, is not a pure spirit and a complete nature, but is naturally ordained to inform a human body and to constitute one individual substance with it. Even though spiritual and immortal by nature, the human soul, in this life, depends in a very large measure on the human body for its operations.

All the Angels are endowed with intellect and free will. No pure spirit is conceivable without these natural faculties. The Angels are commonly called "minds," "intelligences" by theologians and philosophers. Dionysius calls them "celestial intelligences," "intellectual beings," "supercelestial beings," etc. Exalted knowledge and intelligence are the most outstanding qualities of an Angel according to human standards. Thus, in praising David's wisdom, the woman from Thecua could not find a similar intelligence here on earth and compared it to that of an Angelic mind: "Thou, my lord, O King, art wise, according to the wisdom of an Angel of God."[1]

In calling the Angels "minds" and "intelligences" we do not mean to limit the Angelic nature to the intellect but we rather

[1] II Kings 14:20.

wish to stress the power of the Angelic perception, superior by far to our own both in itself and in its mode of operation. We speak here of the natural knowledge of the Angels, the one which is proportioned to their condition of pure spirits; and we abstract, for the time being, from their present condition of comprehensors in which a Godlike, more sublime knowledge is imparted to them through the light of glory. The natural intelligence of an Angel is common to both the good and the fallen angels, the demons. "Although an Angel's intellect is not his own substance, just as our intellects are not our own substances, yet he possesses such penetration, that he is able, at one glance, to take in the whole field of science lying open to his perception, just as we, at a glance, can take in the entire field of vision lying exposed to our eyes."[2]

Our human mind comes into possession of knowledge by a gradual and laborious process. It requires first of all a number of years of physical development for the proper operation. It rises slowly from single sensible perceptions to general ideas of things and finally to abstract truth. The Angelic intellect, entirely free and independent from matter and senses, needs no such development. It is in the full possession of its power from the very beginning of its existence. There is no need of gathering elements of knowledge bit by bit, of adding ideas to ideas in order to discover truth, as is the case with us. Having been created in the full perfection of its nature, the Angelic mind neither develops by gradual growth nor does it suffer any decay; its knowledge does not pass by consecutive steps from the haze of the morning to the splendor of the noonday brightness. From the beginning of its existence it was able to grasp the objects within its own sphere and advert to them without any fatigue in the process, moving in the dazzling light of the purely spiritual world as in its proper element. Its light is not subject to waning into

[2] A. M. Lepicier, *The Unseen World*, p. 27 f.

twilight or disappearing into darkness, as is the case, unfortu-
nately, with the human mind in this life.

Being by nature higher than man and much closer to God, the
Angels receive more of His light, that is, a greater power of
understanding, infused ideas, mind-pictures representing external objects, the spiritual and material creatures of this universe.

The process of Angelic knowing and understanding seems
to consist in a placid gazing on these ideas or mind-pictures
existing within its intellect from the beginning, actuated either
by the Angelic will, or the need of the moment.

There is no room for obscurity or error in the Angelic process
of understanding. Obscurity and doubts often cloud human
knowledge and understanding because of human passions and
the senses. Even though enriched with all the necessary ideas
from the beginning, the Angelic mind is capable of advancing
in knowledge and able to learn about new events, as they occur,
either through Divine Revelation or through illumination from
Angels of a superior Order, or even through men.[3]

We must admit that what we have laid down about Angelic
knowledge and similar questions of the Angelic life are no more
than pure conjectures based on theological and philosophical
principles and a few data of Revelation. "The comprehension of
the Angelic intellect and its mode of operation is a subject of
speculation, concerning which our limited mind is at a decided
disadvantage. The Schoolmen have practically exhausted the
capacity of the human intellect along these lines. As of faith
we need only hold that the Angels are not endowed with
cardiognosis [knowledge of the secrets of the heart] nor with a
certain knowledge of future acts of the free will; these being
exclusively divine prerogatives. It follows that their knowledge

[3] Eph. 3:10.

of the thoughts and future free actions of men is purely conjectural and can at most engender only moral certitude."[4]

The Language of Angels

Do Angels speak and manifest their thoughts to others? It would indeed be inconceivable that such a vast multitude of pure spirits endowed with superior intelligence and an abundance of clear ideas should lack the means of communicating among themselves. Saint Paul speaks of such things as "the tongues of Angels." From Sacred Scripture we learn that Angels do talk with one another;[5] they talk to men every time they are sent as God's messengers into this world. The examples are too many and too obvious: The Archangel Raphael and Tobias, Gabriel the Archangel and Saint Zachary and the Blessed Virgin Mary; an Angel spoke to Saint Peter,[6] etc. If they talk and they sing in a manner and a voice that is not their own, how much more must they be able to talk and sing in the language of the spirits. At the birth of Christ, the heavenly messenger of joy and of great tidings, an Angel of God announced the nativity of the Savior of the world to a few shepherds in the hill country around Bethlehem. Messengers had come down to earth many times since man's creation, to advise, to warn, to help, or to punish man. On this occasion "a multitude of the heavenly army" was heard for the first time singing, caroling, and praising God and saying: "Glory to God in the highest, and on earth peace to men of good will." Only the Angelic mind could well understand the mystery of the Incarnation, and the great honor and dignity that had come to poor human nature when the Son of God, the Eternal Word, assumed and substantially united it to His Divine Person for all eternity.

[4] Pohle-Preuss, *God the Author of Nature and the Supernatural*, p. 317.
[5] Zach. 1:11 ff.   [6] Acts 12:8 f.

The fact that Angels possess a language of their own is beyond all doubt; the nature of that language, however, is little known to us. When the Angels appear to men, a human language is spoken by them, the one spoken by the addressee. The sound of human voice is produced, and human words are spoken when the Angelic apparition is a sensible one; only mental words, the conveying of ideas, are used in cases of imaginative or intellectual visions.

Among themselves the Angels do not converse in any human language, by words of mouth, being incorporeal and immaterial. What is their language then? Of several theories excogitated by the Schoolmen to explain the language of the Angels the one proposed by Saint Thomas seems to be the most acceptable. Saint Thomas holds that the Angels talk to each other by a mere act of the will, opening their mind and revealing whatever ideas they wish to convey to others of the same nature as themselves. This Angelic language, or conversation, is called illumination. Dionysius refers to this mode of speaking where he writes: "The lower orders of the Celestial Beings (the Angels) receive the understanding of the Divine works from those above them in a fitting manner, and the highest are correspondingly enlightened in the Divine Mysteries by the Most High God Himself. For some of them are shown to us enlightened in holy matters by those above them."[7] Dionysius applies to the Angels of higher and lower ranks those questions and replies of Psalm 23, which describe Christ's triumphant ascension into heaven. Some of the Angels are depicted there asking: "Who is this King of glory?" Spirits of the higher Choirs of Angels answer: "The Lord who is strong and mighty, the Lord mighty in battle." Some more Angels ask the same question: "Who is this King of glory?" And the higher Angels reply: "The Lord of hosts, he is the King of glory." "Some of

---

[7] *De Cael. Hier.*, VII.

them," writes Dionysius, "are shown to us enlightened in holy matters by those above them, and [thus] we learn that He who in human form ascended to heaven is Lord of the Celestial Powers and King of glory."[8]

"They [the Angels] need neither tongue nor ears but without the help of any spoken word they exchange with each other their thoughts and their counsels."[9] This form of expression, the Angelic language, may seem perhaps too faint and indistinct to us who are used to material sound and words of mouth; it is however much stronger, clearer, and more perfect than any human language, even when this is used by the most learned and experienced of men. Our words of mouth are no more than symbols of the ideas we have in our mind and wish to manifest to others. Symbols and words are very often inadequate in expressing the full thought, or they are ambiguous or not well understood by the hearer. To be able to open one's mind and reveal the whole thought, as it is there, without the channel of symbolism, sound, and words, is a higher and better form of expression. Such is the wordless exchange of ideas, the language of the Angels.

Just as, by God's permission or command, the Angels are able to assume human forms when appearing to men, so, too, they are permitted to produce a human voice and speak our human language, as all reported Angelic apparitions reveal. By the same Divine permission and in virtue of their natural powers, the Angels are able to produce what to human ears sounds like sweet melody or enchanting music, as we learn from the lives of several of God's servants about whom we shall report later.

The fact of Angelic illumination implies difference of knowledge and ideas between one Angel and another. This difference is determined by the specific degree of perfection of each in-

[8] *Ibid.*
[9] St. John Damascene, *De Fide Orth.*, II, 3.

dividual Angel. Since no two Angels are exactly alike, it follows that their power of understanding and their amount of knowledge differ accordingly. Angelic illumination is needed not only for acquiring new natural ideas but also, and especially, for the supernatural knowledge of the mysteries of God. Here an Angel of the higher ranks, having received more light from God on such mysteries, passes that knowledge along to Angels of lower ranks adjusting himself to their more limited capacity. Saint Paul implies that the Angels can be enlightened on such mysteries even through the Church and human preaching: "To me, the least of all saints is given this grace to preach among the Gentiles, the unsearchable riches of Christ, and to enlighten all men ... that the manifold wisdom of God may be made known to Principalities and Powers in heavenly places through the church."[10]

By opening his mind in light, an Angel is able to reveal not only his thoughts but also his affections, his desires, his joy, his gratitude, his happiness. Such manifestations are immensely more perfect, more beautiful, and convincing than any corresponding human expression. They are a blessed irradiation of whatever sentiment is being expressed. "The first Order of the Celestial Beings," writes Dionysius, "which are established about God, immediately encircling Him, in perpetual purity they encompass His eternal knowledge in that most sublime and eternal Angelic dance, rapt in the bliss of manifold blessed contemplations, and irradiated with pure and primal splendors."[11]

Love and Free Will of the Angels

Free will is an essential constituent of every spiritual nature, divine, angelic, and human. The Angels are pure spirits, as was

[10] Eph. 3:8 ff.
[11] *Op. cit.*, VII.

demonstrated in the preceding chapter. They must consequently enjoy freedom of choice, no less than man who is a little less than the Angels.

Sacred Scripture clearly implies the existence of a free will in the Angelic nature. The mere fact that a number of them sinned while the rest chose to remain loyal to God proves it beyond doubt. Personal sin is a willful transgression of the law of God. Sin cannot exist where there is no free will. Since the Scripture explicitly reveals the sin of the Angels and their banishment from heaven, it clearly implies that they are in possession of a free will. "God spared not the Angels that sinned."[12] "The Angels who kept not their principality, but forsook their own habitation, he hath reserved under darkness in everlasting chains, unto the judgment of the great day."[13] The voluntary abandonment of their "principality" and their subsequent punishment are facts that absolutely presuppose free will and free choice. "An Angel is an intellectual substance, endowed with liberty," writes Saint John Damascene; and again, "Every being that is endowed with reason is also endowed with free will. Consequently an Angel, being a nature endowed with reason and intelligence, is also equipped with freedom of choice. Being a creature, he is mutable, because he is free either to persevere in what is good, or to turn to what is bad."[14]

The words of the Divine Savior revealing that Angels rejoice in heaven when they see a sinner converted to God and doing penance, presuppose a free will and free choice not only in man—the sinner doing penance—but also in the Angels who rejoice instead of lamenting over such an act. "So I say to you, there shall be joy before the Angels of God upon one sinner doing penance."[15] This rejoicing over man's conversion, and hope

---

[12] II Pet. 2:4.   [13] Jude 1:6.
[14] *Op. cit.*, II, 3; St. Thomas Aquinas, *Summa Theo.*, I, Q. 59, art. 3.
[15] Luke 15:10.

of salvation, reveals the most beautiful and noble act of the
Angelic will, their love. They love themselves and each other in
God, and God in Himself and above all else. They love man because he is made to the image and likeness of God, is a partaker
of the Divine nature, redeemed by the Son of God and destined
to live with them in heaven. Yes, they love man, they protect
him, they inspire him with holy thoughts and desires, they offer
his prayers, his good works, his sufferings and his tears to God
and they pray for him. Yes, the good Angels love man as much
as Satan hates him. This love of man explains the heavenly
joy they experience when they see a sinner doing penance, because
through sin he was lost and now has been found, was dead and
has come back to life.

Being entirely free from passions and all sensitive appetites,
the act of the Angelic will is determined exclusively by the
Angelic mind with a decision and a firmness that are final and
admit of no reverse. It was exactly this quality of the Angelic
will, as some say, that made the fallen angels incapable of
conversion and repentance. For an Angel to sin—at the time
of their probation when they were still free to do so—is to assume
an immutable attitude against God, an aversion that will never
end. He thus becomes an adversary of God, a demon. Whereas
the good Angel that has once elicited an act of love of God will
love God for all eternity. "Following that perfect knowledge of
theirs, the Angel's surrender to love is immediate, unwavering,
utterly whole and completely irrevocable. The fire of an Angel's
love is not built up slowly; it has no stages of mere smoldering,
no agonizing moments of dying embers; rather the Angel is
immediately a holocaust, a roaring conflagration, aflame with
a love that will never lessen."[16]

Desire is another manifest sign of a free will in a rational
being. Saint Peter attributes this quality to the will of the Angels.

[16] Walter Farrell, O.P., *Satan—The Devil Himself*, p. 8.

For centuries and ages, ever since the primal revelation was made to them, those heavenly spirits had ardently desired to see the fulfillment of the redemption promised mankind from the beginning: "Into these things Angels desired to look."[17] This desire to see our redemption accomplished is another proof of their love for us.

Once established in grace and admitted to the Beatific Vision, the Angelic will, no less than the human will, can no longer choose between good and evil. The choice it has made of the Good, is now an eternal choice. In the eternal possession of the Supreme Good they can still choose what they please, but their choice is always guided by the love of the Supreme Being and is only a choice between good and better.

Locomotion and Power of the Angels

In order to fully understand the extraordinary power of the Angels it is necessary to know their peculiar relation to space and how they move from one place to another.

An Angel, as every spiritual substance, is said to be present or localized in a particular place not by reason of his own substance being coextended with and circumscribed by space, like material bodies, but merely by virtue of his power being applied to a specific object or a particular place. Being spiritual and completely immaterial he does not fill or occupy space, not even the smallest dimension, not even a single point. His presence in a place is determined, and occasionally made known, by his activity there and not by his substance which has nothing in common with matter.

A graphic example of the presence of an Angel, made known by application of his power, is given in the well-known account of the miraculous cures that took place in the pond called

17 I Pet. 1:12.

Bethsaida, by the Sheepgate of Jerusalem. "An Angel of the Lord descended at certain times into the pond and the water was moved. And he that went down first into the pond after the motion of the water, was made whole, of whatsoever infirmity he lay under."[18] It is not said here that the Angel was ever seen by anybody when coming into that pond. His presence became manifest only by his action of stirring the waters and giving health to the first infirm person entering the pond.

The action of the Angel that determines his presence may affect material objects or immaterial subjects, like the human soul, other Angels, or demons.

Being thus engaged in one place the Angel cannot exert his activity and thereby be present at another place at the same time. He can be present and operate in one place at a time, and cannot reach by one action various objects in separate places. However, Angels pass from one place to another with the rapidity of thought. Their motion is not really a locomotion but merely an instantaneous change of place, even when the local distance between the second place and the first is of several thousand miles. His motion consists in transferring his attention and activity from one object to another without having to pass successively through the intermediate places and space. He can, however, follow a continuous motion through space when his activity demands it. Our mind, the closest thing to an Angel, even without leaving the location occupied by our body, travels with the speed of a spirit. At a moment's notice I can transfer my thoughts and my imagination from one continent to another, visit friends and even, perhaps, affect them telepathically. What a man can do mentally only, an Angel can do by actually transferring his own self and all his activity from one continent to another with the speed of lightning or, better, the speed of thought.

[18] John 5:4.

It is recorded in the Bible that on such flights the Angels have transported material objects or human beings with the same speed of spirit motion. An excellent example of this is found in the book of Daniel. For six days the Prophet Daniel was in the den of lions without being touched by the hungry felines kept there. During those days the Lord remembered Daniel and sent an Angel to bring him food. The Angel had to provide real food somewhere on earth and then bring it to Daniel. Daniel was in Babylon; the Angel went to Judea, some six hundred miles west of Babylon, and this is how he did it: "There was in Judea a prophet called Habacuc, and he had boiled pottage, and had broken bread in a bowl, and was going into the field, to carry it to the reapers. And the Angel of the Lord said to Habacuc: Carry the dinner which thou hast into Babylon to Daniel, who is in the lions' den. And Habacuc said: Lord, I never saw Babylon, nor do I know the den. And the Angel of the Lord took him by the top of his head, and carried him by the hair of his head, and set him in Babylon over the den in the force of his spirit. And Habacuc cried saying: O Daniel, thou servant of God, take the dinner that God hath sent thee. . . . And Daniel arose and ate. And the Angel of the Lord presently set Habacuc again in his own place."[19]

The mode of Angelic locomotion is clearly expressed in those words: "in the force of his spirit." A locomotion that does not pass successively through the intermediate spaces is implied there where the Scripture says that "the Angel of the Lord *presently* (that is, that very moment, immediately) set Habacuc again in his own place." It is not said that Habacuc was carried all the way back to his place, but that he was set, placed again in his place six hundred miles away, still in time to prepare another meal for his reapers. It is not conceivable that the Angel who

[19] Dan. 14:32-38.

provided Daniel with food should let the poor laborers in the field go hungry.

An Angel is a finite being, a creature, and as such he cannot perform miracles. A miracle, in the strict sense of the word "is something done by God outside the order of all created nature."[20] God is the principal cause of every miracle. He may—and usually does—make use of creatures, as Angels and Saints, as instrumental causes of miracles. However, many effects produced by Angels, according to their own natural powers, may appear like miracles to us because of the extraordinary manner in which they are produced and because of the superior power they reveal, but in fact they are not real miracles but Angelic deeds. The amazing swiftness of their movements, the devastating power of destruction which they manifest when God employs them as avenging Angels, are in reality ordinary exploits of the Angelic nature; yet they appear like miracles to us.

A classical example of Angelic avenging power has been recorded in the Bible. One single Angel of the Lord wiped out a whole army of Assyrian warriors in one night. Led by Sennacherib, the Assyrians had come to take Jerusalem in the days of King Ezechias. At the prayers of the pious King, the Lord promised to protect the city of Jerusalem and not to permit the Assyrians to shoot a single arrow into the city. The Lord gave the avenging mission to one of His Angels. "And it came to pass that night, that an Angel of the Lord came, and slew in the camp of the Assyrians a hundred and eighty-five thousand. And when he arose early in the morning, he saw all the bodies of the dead."[21] This extraordinary historical event is recorded in four different books of the Scripture and finds its confirmation in the history books of Josephus Flavius and of Herodotus. The inspired writers tell us what the Lord revealed to them,

---

[20] *Summa Theo.*, I, Q. 110, art. 4.
[21] IV Kings 19:35; Tob. 1:21; Ecclus. 48:24; Isa. 37:36.

namely that an Angel did it all. The pagan writers tell us how that mysterious agent accomplished it, namely making use of natural destructive means, deadly microbes and bacteria causing a plague: "God had sent a pestilential distemper upon his (Sennacherib's) army; and on the very first night of the siege, a hundred four score and five thousand, with their captains and generals were destroyed."[22]

The hand of the avenging Angel appears manifest in this incident which reminds us of the plagues of Egypt, in the days of Moses, when the Lord must have made extensive use of the Angelic ministry in producing those great signs and portents.

"The phenomena to which the power of Angels may give rise, whether exercised mediately or immediately, must be of a remarkable character, both as regards their extent and their diversity. As on the one hand these pure spirits possess a knowledge of physical and chemical laws far surpassing our own knowledge, and as on the other their power is of such vast range, we must assume that there are hardly any phenomena in the world which they cannot produce in one way or another. Indeed, such effects may be so surprising as to have all the appearances of miracles. They are not, however, true miracles, for, though they surpass the powers of the visible universe, so far as it is known to us, they do not in reality surpass the powers of the Angelic nature, a miracle being due to the power of God alone, and surpassing all the powers both of visible and invisible nature."[23]

Among the many effects of the Angelic power we must mention that of assuming a visible form or the appearance of a human body, always with God's permission or command. The many corporeal apparitions of Angels and Archangels mentioned in the Bible need not be repeated here. However, those assumed

---

[22] *Antiquitates Judaicae*, X, I, 5; *History*, II, 41.
[23] Lepicier, *op. cit.*, p. 66 f.

bodies do not become part of their nature. They are used merely as necessary instruments for communicating visibly with men. They are not real bodies, and whatever vital actions they seem to perform with them are such only in appearance. "I seemed indeed to eat and to drink with you," said the Archangel Raphael, "but I use an invisible meat and drink, which cannot be seen by men."[24] The non-reality of the Archangel's assumed body was made manifest by his sudden vanishing into thin air: "And when he (the Archangel) had said these things, he was taken from their sight, and they could see him no more."[25]

[24] Tob. 12:19.
[25] *Ibid.*, 21.

Chapter III

THE SONS OF GOD AND THE SONS OF PERDITION

Grace of God and Probation

THE Angels, the first creatures of the universe, were created to God's own image and similitude. "The Angel," writes Saint Thomas, "is the most excellent of all creatures because among all creatures he bears the greatest resemblance to his Creator. The glossa on Ezechiel, 28, *Thou wast the seal of resemblance*, says: The more subtle their nature (the Angelic nature) the better is the image of God found expressed in them."[1] The Lord bestowed on them marvelous gifts of nature and grace: wisdom, power, beauty, holiness. With the supernatural gift of sanctifying grace, He infused in them all the virtues of faith, hope, and charity and the gifts of the Holy Ghost. Thus their natural life of created spirits was divinely perfected. The Angels became sharers and participants of the Divine Life and were given the opportunity to merit the reward of eternal bliss in the face-to-face vision of God in heaven. Thus the morning stars of creation became the first adoptive sons of God.

Saint Thomas believes that the Angels were given all these supernatural virtues and gifts of grace (which are absolutely necessary to every intelligent creature who would attain Beatific Vision) in exact proportion to their individual natural aptitude and perfection.[2] Since the natural perfection of one Angel differs specifically from that of any other, it would follow that the

[1] *Opusc.* 60, I.   [2] *Summa Theo.* I, Q. 52, art. 6.

degrees of grace among the Angels differ even more than among our Saints, according to St. Thomas.

That the Angels were actually elevated to the supernatural order and endowed with sanctifying grace is a truth firmly and unanimously defended by Catholic Theologians. This truth is based on Divine Revelation where the Angels are often called "saints,"[3] "sons of God,"[4] "Angels of light"[5] in opposition to Satan. They are portrayed as enjoying Beatific Vision: "Their Angels in heaven always see the face of my Father who is in heaven."[6] To this vision they could be admitted only because they had been previously sanctified and had persevered in grace.

The sanctity of the Angels, no less than that of man, is not a quality of nature, nor anything demanded by nature, but a supernatural gift of God, freely bestowed out of that same divine love which had freely given them all the gifts of nature and nature itself. "The Powers of heaven (the Angels) are not holy by nature, but they possess the measure of their sanctification from the Holy Spirit, according to the rank by which one excels another."[7] According to Saint Augustine, the gift of grace was bestowed upon the Angels together with the gift of nature, so that their creation and their sanctification were simultaneous: "God created the Angels with a chaste love whereby they adhered to Him, granting to them His grace while creating their nature."[8]

The exact time of the sanctification of the Angels is not a matter of faith. But Saint Augustine's opinion on this has become the prevailing one, especially since the time Saint Thomas defended it against some medieval theologians who maintained that the Angels remained for some time in the pure

---

[3] Dan. 8:13.
[4] Job 1:6; 2:1; 38:7.
[5] II Cor. 11:14.
[6] Matt. 18:10.
[7] St. Basil, *De Spiritu Sancto,* XVI, 38.
[8] *De Civitate Dei,* XII, 9.

state of nature and were elevated to the supernatural order some time later. Saint Augustine's opinion has been adopted by the Roman Catechism.

Just like man, the Angels had to undergo a period of probation during which they were free to choose between good and evil. They were not yet confirmed in grace and they did not enjoy the Beatific Vision during this time. This was a period of existence like that of our first parents before their fall, insofar as they were wayfarers, living in faith and hope of those supernal truths and promises that God had revealed to them. During this time the Angels had the great opportunity to merit heaven and eternal life with God, but in the meantime they were exposed to the danger of committing sin and thereby losing God and heaven for all eternity. The Fathers and the theologians are unanimous in admitting a period of probation for the Angels. Gennadius, who disagreed with them, asserted that the Angels were created in a state of grace and glory. His opinion would suppose that sin is possible for those who enjoy Beatific Vision. The freedom of choosing what is evil or wrong does no longer exist in the state of glory.

It is matter of faith that during their period of probation some of the Angels sinned and were condemned to hell. The fact that they did sin proves that there was a time in their existence when sin was possible. Since they could not sin *in statu termini* (the state of final consummation which excludes the possibility of further merit or demerit) they must have sinned *in statu viae* (the state of wayfaring or probation). This state is necessarily a state of faith and not of vision, of merit not of reward. Hence the existence of such a state of probation for the Angels is a firm theological conclusion.

How long did this probation last? Divine Revelation offers no answer to this question. The various opinions expressed on the subject by some theologians are pure speculations. They speak of one single instant, or the time required for the first act of love elicited by the Angels;[9] or of two or three instants, or *morulae*,[10] the first instant marking the act of creation and sanctification, the second referring to their perseverance or fall, the third to their reception into the glory of heaven or their damnation. Since we do not even know how long the period of probation of our first parents was, we should not presume to define the duration of the test imposed by the Lord on His Angels.

Considering the great difference existing between the Angelic nature and the human, and between their respective mode of operation, it would seem *a priori* that the Angels would require a much shorter period of probation than man. Man is relatively very slow in his physical development and in his mental operations. The Angel is in full possession of his natural gifts from the very beginning, and his mental process is instantaneous and perfect. Divine grace perfects nature according to the proper mode of that nature, hence the Angelic nature would seem to have required a much shorter time than man's nature both for its perfecting and for its testing. However, these considerations do not take into account the hidden reasons of Divine Providence which could have demanded a much longer period of probation for the Angels, because the period of probation is also a period of merit. The fact that the first act of love of God elicited by the good Angels merited heaven for them, does not seem a sufficient reason to prove that they were immediately admitted to the glory of heaven. They could have merited more glory by being given the opportunity for more such meritorious acts: "He that is just, let him be justified still; and he that is holy, let him be sanctified still."[11] Man who is in the state of grace is not taken immediately into heaven after eliciting his first act

[9] *Summa Theo.*, I, Q. 62, art. 5.
[10] Franciscus Suarez, S.J., *De Angelis*, VI, 3, 5.
[11] Apoc. 22:11.

of love of God but he is left ordinarily a long time here on earth in his state of probation in order that he may acquire more merit. Something analogous must have been the case with the probation of the Angels.

One thing distinguishes man's probation from that of the Angels. The first act of love of God elicited by an Angel is a final choice; he will love God forever. We may say that thereby he is practically confirmed in grace, for he who will never deflect from the love of God will never lose His grace. On the other hand the Angel who sins will sin forever. He is lost: "Because of his exalted perfection an Angel who sins falls far; because of the perfection of the angelic will the Angel who falls, falls but once."[12] Their first choice of good or evil is an immutable, an eternal choice. After this choice Angels are divided not simply into saints and sinners, as it is usually the case with men (who after their fall are given an opportunity for conversion, redemption, and salvation), but into good Angels and Devils.

Another outstanding difference between the period of probation of the Angels and that of man is this, that all the Angels were individually and personally subjected to their probation, because they were all there at the time; whereas only the first parents, the first father and mother, were personally present when all mankind was subjected to a test. With the fall of Adam all mankind fell, because all mankind was virtually present in him and actually represented by him through a divine decree. Hence, because Adam sinned we all sinned. Only a number of the Angels fell, because only a number of them disobeyed and sinned; the others, the great majority of them, undismayed by the bad example given by some of their brethren, remained loyal to God, clinging to Him with pure and ardent love. The good Angels never knew sin, but all men (except Jesus our

---

[12] Walter Farrell, O.P., *Satan—The Devil Himself*, p. 14.

Lord and His Immaculate Mother) because of original sin are servants of sin, children of wrath and in need of redemption. This sinlessness of the good Angels, more than their exalted nature, renders them so wonderful and so lovable to us, and so dear to God.

The Heavenly Hierarchies and the Choirs of Angels

As has already been explained, the Angels are pure spirits, incorporeal and in every sense immaterial substances. There is no question of generation and multiplication with them, consequently no angelic families and clans. Each Angel stands apart as a complete and direct creation of God. Each Angel, according to Saint Thomas, is specifically different from any other in the entire spirit world, so that he possesses more or less perfection than the one next to him, by a degree higher or lower than that which here below separates man from a brute animal, an animal from a plant. This is because each Angel is a pure form. Now, every differentiation in form implies differentiation in species. Human beings, no matter what their race, belong all to one and the same species. They differ only individually by some material or moral quality that does not alter substantially their specific nature of a rational creature composed of body and soul.

The Lord of heaven Who has grouped the children of men according to races, tribes, families, and nations must have assigned some order to the more numerous and more diversiform world of the Angels. The various names, in the plural number, given to the Angels in the Bible seem to imply that there are various orders and ranks among them. What is said here of the Choirs and Hierarchies of the Angels is not an article of faith, yet it should be regarded as a certain truth.

As a matter of fact the Scripture mentions nine different orders of Angels. In various passages in the Old and New Testa-

ment mention is made of Seraphim, Cherubim, Thrones, Dominations, Principalities, Powers, Virtues, Archangels, and Angels.[13] The mere fact that the Scripture carefully distinguishes
between these various names of Angelic orders is sufficient
reason to believe that they actually represent different ranks in
the spirit world, with a difference of perfection and of office between the various orders of Angels. There seems to be no basis
whatever to the opinion that these nine different denominations
are synonymous terms. It never happens that while the Scripture
is talking, for example, of Seraphim it would next refer to them
as Thrones, Dominations, etc. The only exception is to be made
with the term Angel, which is used both as a specific term for the
lowest Choir, and as generic term for all the Choirs, as when the
Psalmist says: "Praise ye him, all his angels; praise ye him,
all his hosts."[14] "All his angels" here means all the choirs of
Angels, whatever their name and their rank.

Some writers believe that this enumeration of nine Choirs of
Angels is incomplete, because of the following words of Saint
Paul: "Above all principality, and power, and virtue, and
dominion and every name that is named, not only in this world,
but also in that which is to come."[15] They say that "every name
that is named" would seem to imply an indefinite number of
Angelic Orders. While this is true, those same words could
be equally well explained by the fact that in this passage Saint
Paul had mentioned only four out of nine Choirs, hence those
words could also imply that the enumeration just given is incomplete.

There is a great disagreement and uncertainty in Patristic
tradition on this point. Except for Saint Ambrose and Dionysius,
(Saint Gregory the Great and Saint John Damascene both de-

[13] Isa. 6:2; Gen. 3:24; Col. 1:6; Eph. 1.21; Rom. 8:38.
[14] Ps. 148:2.
[15] Eph. 1:21.

pend upon Dionysius in this matter), the theory of the nine Choirs and the Angelic Hierarchies is unknown to the Greek and Latin Fathers. They hardly ever agree in either the number and the names of the Angelic Orders.[16] A diligent analysis of the Scripture, however, gives us the nine orders and names of Angels: "We say that there are nine orders of Angels, because we know from Scripture to be so," says Saint Gregory.[17]

In the days of Saint Gregory the theory of the nine Choirs of Angels was well established because of the accepted authority of Pseudo Dionysius the Areopagite. However, as far back as the days of Saint Ignatius Martyr, who died 107 A.D., explicit mention is made of hierarchies and of ranks of Angels: "I am in chains and able to grasp heavenly things, the ranks of the angels, the hierarchy of principalities, things visible and invisible."[18] Saint Ambrose enumerates the nine Choirs of Angels in ascending order from Angels to Seraphim, without any hesitation.[19] Saint Augustine, on the contrary, candidly admits his ignorance regarding any difference between the Angelic orders. Commenting on Colossians, chapter 1:16, *whether thrones, or dominations, or principalities, or powers,* he writes: "What difference is there between these four terms ... let those tell who can, I for myself must confess that I do not know."[20] Several of the Fathers believe that the enumeration of the Angelic orders found in the Scripture is incomplete. Commenting on Psalm 135, Saint Hilary writes that the Apostle Paul either purposely concealed or he ignored the exact number of Angelic Choirs. Saint Jerome seizes on the same idea. After referring to one of the enumerations given by Saint Paul, he adds the following: "And the other terms of ministry which neither we

[16] F. Prat, S.J., *The Theology of St. Paul,* Vol. II, p. 415 f.
[17] *Hom. 34 in Evang.*
[18] *Epistle to the Trallians,* 5.
[19] *Apologia Proph. David,* 5.
[20] *Enchiridion,* 58.

ourselves nor Paul himself, I believe, was able to name while still in his mortal body."[21] Saint Jerome enumerates only seven Choirs of Angels, but he insists on a real difference between them: "Why do we read that in the kingdom of heaven there are Archangels, Angels, Thrones, Dominions, Powers, Cherubim and Seraphim, and every name which is named not only in this present world, but also that which is to come? A difference of name is meaningless where there is not a difference of rank. An Archangel is of course an Archangel to other inferior Angels, and Powers and Dominions have other spheres over which they exercise authority."[22] The wavering and unsettled opinion about the Choirs of Angels, before the days of Dionysius, appears very manifest in the *Apostolic Constitutions,* which, at one time (in the Mass Clementina, VIII, 12), mentions ten Angelic Choirs, including *Aeons* and *Hosts* but omitting Dominions; at another time it lists eleven Choirs, adding Dominions to the previous enumeration.

Saint John Damascene seems to attribute the final decision on the matter of Choirs and Hierarchies to his predecessor Dionysius: "As the most holy and venerable man and excellent theologian Denis the Areopagite says, the entire theology, that is Sacred Scripture, has listed nine celestial substances which our master theologian has divided in three orders (hierarchies)."[23] It is evident that the merit of Dionysius is limited to the division of the nine Choirs into three Hierarchies. The Choirs themselves and their names are found in Sacred Scripture, and they had been grouped together long before the time of Dionysius by, for example, Saint Ambrose. With the translation of his works into Latin his theory of the nine Choirs and the three Hierarchies became the commonly accepted opinion also in the

[21] *Contra Jovinianum,* II, 28.
[22] *Ibid.*
[23] *De Fide Ortho.,* 2, 3.

West. Beginning with the most perfect Hierarchy and the highest Choirs of Angels, the Angelic world is thus divided according to Dionysius:

I. THE SUPREME HIERARCHY
Seraphim—Cherubim—Thrones
II. MIDDLE HIERARCHY
Dominations—Virtues—Powers
III. LOWER HIERARCHY
Principalities—Archangels—Angels

These nine orders of Angels are commonly called Choirs. Because the word choir means a band of singers, it is liable to create a wrong notion about the number and the duties of the Angels. Singing the praises of the Most High is indeed one of the most pleasant and desired occupation of all celestial spirits, but certainly not the only duty and occupation. Their vast number of countless millions and myriads in each Choir would be better expressed by other terms, like Order, Rank, Hosts, etc. Yet, the accepted name should be retained because of its antiquity.

What is meant by Angelic Hierarchy? According to Dionysius, in this case Hierarchy implies a holy order, a special knowledge, and a specific activity which, so far as possible, "participates in the Divine Likeness and is lifted up to the illuminations given it from God, and correspondingly towards the imitation of God. . . . The aim of the Hierarchy is the greatest possible assimilation to and union with God. . . . Also it molds and perfects its participants in the holy image of God like bright and spotless mirrors which receive the ray of the supreme Deity which is the source of light, and being mystically filled with the gift of light, it pours it forth again abundantly, in accordance with God's law, upon those below itself."[24]

[24] *The Celestial Hierarchies*, 3.

Hierarchy, a sacred authority, generally speaking, implies some common sphere of activity and influence; Orders, among Angels, imply gradual rank of both natural perfection and supernatural grace and glory. This is the meaning of Saint Bernard's consideration: "The citizens of that country are spirits, mighty, glorious, blessed, separate personalities, of gradual rank, from the beginning standing in their own order, perfect of their kind."[25]

As we have noted before, all the names of the Angelic Orders, or Choirs, are found in Sacred Scripture; they are not an invention of Dionysius. The distribution of the nine Choirs into three distinct Hierarchies is a theory he derived ultimately from Neo-Platonic Philosophy prevalent in his time. According to Proclus: "The progressions of beings are completed through similitude. However, the terminations of the higher orders are united to the beginnings of second orders . . . and thus all things are in continuity with each other."[26] Dionysius develops these basic ideas both in his Celestial and Ecclesiastical Hierarchies. He confesses his inability to give us a clear picture of that wondrous organization of the Angelic world when he writes: "I hold that none but the Divine Creator, by whom they were ordained, is able to know fully the number and the nature of the celestial Beings and the regulation of their Hierarchies. . . . We could not have known the mystery of these supercelestial Intelligences and all the holiness of their perfection had it not been taught to us by God through His ministers who truly know their own natures. Therefore we will say nothing as from ourselves, but being instructed we will set forth, according to our ability, those angelic visions which the venerable theologians have beheld."[27]

[25] *De Consideratione*, V, 4.
[26] *The Philosophy of Plato*, VI, 2.
[27] *Op. cit.*, VI.

According to Dionysius, a Hierarchy is a threefold order and a co-equal unity. The most exalted Hierarchy, that of the Orders of Seraphim, Cherubim, and Thrones, is the most fully Godlike, the most closely and immediately united to the first Light of the Godhead.[28]

The first and the second Hierarchy possess all the illumination and the power of the lower Hierarchy, that of the Principalities, the Archangels, and the Angels. This, according to Dionysius, is the reason why all the blessed spirits, including those of the highest Choirs, are rightly called Angels—the name of the lowest Choir—because they all possess, in addition to their own personal perfection, the illumination and the power of the common Angel, but the Angels themselves do not participate equally with those above them.

It is well known how the concept of the heavenly Hierarchy was accommodated, by the same author, to the Ecclesiastical Hierarchy. Here, too, a member of the highest Order, a Bishop, has all the sacred power and sacred knowledge of any member of the lower Orders, the Priests, the Deacons, etc., but these do not share equally with him in that power. The Angelic Choirs, or Orders, exercise their power by means of illumination and purgation, enriching and perfecting the Angelic or human intelligences that are immediately below themselves according to their receptive capacity. By analogy, the same functions of purging, illuminating, and perfecting are attributed to the various Orders of the Ecclesiastical Hierarchy by Dionysius. This is indeed a very harmonious and beautiful conception of God's family in heaven and on earth, a family in which all are joined together in charity among themselves and all are united in God with divine love.

"The first Hierarchy of the celestial Intelligences is purified and enlightened, being ordained by the first perfecting Cause,

[28] *Ibid.*

uplifted directly to Himself, and filled, analogously, with the most holy purification of the boundless light of the supreme perfection, untouched by any inferiority, full of primal light and perfected by its union with the first-given understanding and knowledge."[29] According to this principle, the Choirs of the first Hierarchy receive, in proportion to their Order and personal perfection, illumination and purgation directly from God; the others indirectly, that is, through the members of the Choir and Hierarchy immediately above them, except, of course, for the supernatural light of grace and glory which is given to all directly from God.

It is practically beyond our power of comprehension and comparison to balance one against the other, the highest in the Order of Seraphim with the lowest in the Choir of Angels, in the third Hierarchy. The highest in the Choir of Seraphim must have been the most brilliant, most perfect and glorious creature of the spirit world, a bearer of light and beauty, the ideal of creation. According to Sacred Scripture the apostasy of the fallen Angels must be attributed to one of the most exalted spirits. He sinned by pride and seduced the others by his example and his lies.[30]

The Fallen Angels

We have an eye-witness account of the fall of this supreme Angel in the words of Christ, the Son of God: "I saw Satan like lightning falling from heaven."[31] What happened to this towering glory of creation to fall so low from such an exalted position? The same Divine Savior reveals something of the cause of his fall: "He was a murderer from the beginning, and he stood not in truth; because truth is not in him. When he speaketh

[29] *Ibid.*
[30] *Summa Theo.*, I, Q. 63, art. 7.
[31] Luke 10:18.

a lie, he speaketh of his own: for he is a liar, and the father thereof."[32] He is called a murderer, from the beginning, because he destroyed, by his example and seduction, the life of grace in his fellow Angels and, later, in our first parents; he is depicted as the great liar, because blinded by pride he attributed to himself those marvelous gifts that God had graciously and most generously showered on him. To him, therefore, the words of Isaias have been aptly applied, and Lucifer has become a synonym of Satan: "How art thou fallen from heaven, O Lucifer, who didst rise in the morning? how art thou fallen to the earth? ... And thou saidst in thy heart: I will ascend into heaven. I will exalt my throne above the stars of God ... I will ascend above the height of the clouds, I will be like the most High. But yet thou shalt be brought down to hell, into the depth of the pit."[33] These words of Isaias are a parable alluding directly to the King of Babylon but indirectly to Satan whose spirit and actions were reflected in that King's conduct. Another tyrannical ruler, the King of Tyre, gives Prophet Ezechiel the opportunity for another description of Satan before and after his fall: "Thus saith the Lord God: Thou wast the seal of resemblance, full of wisdom, and perfect in beauty. Thou wast in the pleasures of the paradise of God. Every precious stone was thy covering: the sardius, the topaz, and the jasper, the chrysolite, and the onyx, and the beryl, the sapphire, and the carbuncle, and the emerald: gold the work of thy beauty, and thy pipes were prepared in the day that thou wast created. Thou a Cherub stretched out, and protecting, and I set thee in the holy mountain of God, thou hast walked in the midst of the stones of fire. Thou wast perfect in thy ways from the day of thy creation, until iniquity was found in thee ... thou hast sinned, and I cast thee

---

[32] John 8:44.

[33] Isa. 14:12 ff. Other names for Satan in Hebrew tradition are: Belial (II Cor. 6:15), Beelzebub (Luke 11:15), Asmodeus (Tob. 3:8), and Sammael (Ascension of Isaias, II).

out from the mountain of God, and destroyed thee, O covering Cherub, out of the midst of the stones of fire. And thy heart was lifted up with thy beauty: thou hast lost thy wisdom in thy beauty, I have cast thee to the ground."[34]

The name Lucifer, the comparison with the Cherubim, the exalted beauty and wisdom of this spirit before his fall, all these seem to be sufficient indications leading to the conclusion that Satan, most probably, was the supreme Angel in the Choir of Cherubim.

Both Fathers and Theologians quite generally hold that the sin of the fallen angels was pride. Pride is a false estimation of oneself; it is a lie, just as humility is truth. Pride is the root of disobedience, the instigator of seditions and rebellions. In that period of probation one of the supreme Angels recognized his exceeding power, beauty, and knowledge but failed to give thanks and glory to God. He became envious and intolerant of God's supreme dominion and thereby he constituted himself as the adversary of God: he became *Satan*. Like a sinister flash of lightning his evil mind was made manifest in the spirit world. Because of his exalted position many Angels followed him in his mad campaign of hate and rebellion. It was then that a cry and a challenge was heard in the heavens, and a leader was seen to rise from the lowest Hierarchy, from the Choir of the Archangels. His battle cry: *"Who is like God?"* was his mighty weapon and it became, later, his own name: *Michael.* "And there was a great battle in heaven, Michael and his Angels fought with the dragon, and the dragon fought and his Angels. And they prevailed not, neither was their place found any more in heaven. And that great dragon was cast out, that old serpent, who is called the devil and Satan, who seduceth the whole world; and he was cast down unto the earth, and his angels were thrown down with him."[35]

[34] Ezech. 28:12 ff.   [35] Apoc. 12:7 ff.

Just as the Archangel Michael earned his name in the battle of heaven, so did Satan acquire his by the defying attitude he took against God. *Satan* in Hebrew means the "adversary," the "accuser." The Greek version of the Septuagint translates *Satan* with *Diabolos,* hence the Latin *Diabolus,* and all the derived vernacular names, including the English term "Devil." The Devil is therefore the equivalent of Satan, the leader of the fallen angels. The other fallen angels have no proper name but they are called either "evil spirits," "spirits of wickedness," "unclean spirits," or simply "devils," because of their association with Satan their leader who is known as "The Devil." Another name, applied to fallen angels, is common to both Sacred Scripture and pagan literature: the term "demon," from the Greek *Daimon.* The Greeks, like Socrates, distinguished between good and bad *daimones.* In the Bible the word demon has always the meaning of an evil being. The false gods of the Gentiles are called demons: "All the gods of the Gentiles are devils."[36] Beelzebub, one of the various names of Satan, is called "the prince of demons."[37]

Evil, in this world and in all of God's creation, begins with Satan and his associates. "The Devil and all the other demons, as created by God, were naturally good, but they did become evil by their own doing."[38] All the wickedness and the resulting suffering, misery, and death in this world can be traced back to Satan. He, the old serpent, who is called the devil and Satan, "seduced Eve by his subtlety."[39] This was the beginning of man's fall, ruin, and death: "For God created man incorruptible, and to the image of his own likeness he made him, but by the envy of the devil, death came into the world."[40]

[36] Ps. 95:5.
[37] Luke 11:15.
[38] IV Lateran Council, c. "Firmiter." D. 428.
[39] II Cor. 11:3.
[40] Wisd. 2:23 f.

"From the psychological point of view," writes J. Pohle, "it is a reasonable assumption that the apostasy of the Angels was instigated by one of their own number, most likely by the one who ranked highest both in natural and supernatural endowment, and that consequently the kingdom of evil originated at the very summit of creation and thence spread over heaven and earth."[41]

The devil sinned with perfect knowledge and complete freedom, without any bad example or seduction, consequently his sin was inexcusable. With the exception of Salmeron and very few others, the theologians believe that, unlike man, Satan and the fallen angels were given no time for repentance. This opinion seems to be firmly based on the words of the Scripture that reveal the fall of the angels, like: "God spared not the angels that sinned, but delivered them, drawn down by infernal ropes to the lower hell, unto torments, to be reserved unto judgment."[42] In these words, like in the following ones taken from the Apocalypse, there seems to be no time left between sin and punishment, the punishment being eternal damnation and the torments of hell. "Michael and the Angels fought with the dragon, and the dragon fought and his angels; and they prevailed not, neither was their place found any more in heaven."[43]

It has been pointed out before that perhaps one third of all the inhabitants of the spirit world followed the example of Satan and were expelled from heaven with him: "His tail (the dragon's) drew the third part of the stars of heaven, and cast them to the earth."[44]

There were defections, probably, from almost every Choir of the heavenly Hierarchies. Saint Paul mentions Principalities and Powers among the fallen angels, who try to seduce man with their deceits: "Put you on the armor of God, that you may be

[41] *God the Author of Nature and the Supernatural*, p. 342.
[42] II Pet. 2:4.   [43] Apoc. 12:7 f.   [44] *Ibid*. 4.

able to stand against the deceits of the devil. For our wrestling is not against flesh and blood, but against Principalities and Powers, against the rulers of the world of this darkness, against the spirits of wickedness in the high places."[45] As Saint Paul never gives a complete enumeration of all the Choirs of the good Angels at one time, we may surmise that he follows the same rule with the fallen angels. The mention of Principalities and Powers in this passage should not be taken as complete and exclusive, but only as more representative and as implying the great natural power and cunning of our adversaries. Even though deprived of all supernatural grace and superadded gifts, the fallen angels retain their natural power which, in itself, is far superior to the natural power of man. For this reason the Apostle demands that the faithful put on the "armor of God" and "the shield of faith" in order to be able to resist and to conquer. Yet, in view of the fact that in another list of fallen angels, the Apostle mentions again only these two Choirs: Principalities and Powers, we believe that the largest number of fallen angels must have come from them. Speaking of Christ's victory over sin and the Devil, Saint Paul says: "Despoiling the Principalities and Powers, he hath exposed them confidently in open show, triumphing over them in himself."[46]

With the fall of Satan and his angels, the good Angels closed their ranks: "Neither was their place (Satan's and associates') found any more in heaven." It was then, we believe, that the good Angels who had stood their test and devoted themselves irrevocably to God's service and love, were admitted to their eternal reward in the glory of heaven and began to enjoy the Beatific Vision without fear of ever losing it. The heaven in which the big battle took place between Michael and Satan was

[45] Eph. 6:11. In the book of Henoch, VI, 7, 8, the number of the fallen angels is put at two hundred only.

[46] Col. 2:15.

not the heaven of glory and Beatific Vision, but the heaven of the spirit world during the period of probation; for no sin is possible in the land of the Blessed nor war in the house of peace.

The good Angels became the court of the most High King of Heaven, God's army against all the legions of the rebel spirits, and God's messengers to men.

It was here on earth, after man's creation and fall, that the good Angels met their fallen comrades of old. On many occasions Satan's path crossed that of Michael the Archangel. One of these occasions has been revealed and recorded for us by the Apostle Saint Jude: "When Michael the Archangel, disputing with the Devil, contended about the body of Moses, he did not venture to accuse him insultingly; he was content to say, May the Lord rebuke thee."[47]

The war against God has been taken down to earth and directed against man. The Angels of heaven can sin no more and Satan would waste his time trying to seduce them now. But man, who even after his fall, has a chance for conversion and salvation, because of Christ's redemptive work for him, can be made to fall again and again until he rises no more and is lost. The Devil who was "a murderer from the beginning" has continued his murderous activity with the children of man. Ever since original sin he has exercised a reign of death—the *imperium mortis*—over mankind, so that in a spiritual sense he became "the prince of this world" by making man the slave of sin. Satan with the assistance of his demons extends this "reign of death" in three principal manners: by seductive temptations; by diabolical obsessions and possessions; by all sorts of black magic, spiritism, and the superstitions of idolatry.

The reality of diabolical activity in this world is so plainly and so strongly emphasized in the Scriptures of both Testaments that it would be superfluous for us to prove it. The diabolical

[47] Jude 1:9.

perversity and cruelty, manifested by so many people in this present generation, living in the most enlightened period of human history, cannot be explained without the presence, in our midst, of an evil genius who delights in man's suffering and despair. This unseen evil genius is Satan. But why hate man? The obvious answer is that Satan hates God and anyone made to His image; much more so since God Himself assumed a human nature. Some theologians believe that one of the reasons of Satan's rebellion and disobedience was the fact that God revealed to the Angels the great things He had in store for man, elevation to the supernatural order, the Incarnation of the Son of God and the Hypostatic Union, the Virgin Mother of God, Mary. God commanded all the Angels to adore the Incarnate Word, as Saint Paul writes: "When He bringeth in the first begotten into the world, He saith: And let all the Angels of God adore him."[48] Envy and pride were, it seems, the cause of Satan's rebellion and fall. Man reminds him always of his fall and his misery, hence his hatred and the relentless campaign against man with the intention of making him an associate of his own misery and despair. This campaign will last to the end of the world. At the final Judgment, Satan, his demons, and all lost souls will hear the eternal condemnation already announced by Christ: "Depart from me, you cursed, into everlasting fire which was prepared for the devil and his angels."[49] No repentance, therefore, and no salvation for the Devil, the adversary and the enemy of God, as, once, Origen and, lately, G. Papini[50] dared to affirm.

Many other problems are connected with the fallen angels, but they belong to a different treatise, to Demonology. Our task, at present, is limited to the good Angels and their activity in this world.

[48] Hebr. 1:6.   [49] Matt. 25:41.   [50] *Il Diavolo,* 1953.

Chapter IV

ANGELS AND THEIR NAMES

The Common Names

WHETHER or not every Angel has a proper name whereby he is distinguished from other heavenly spirits of the same Order or Choir we do not know. Each name that Scripture and Tradition have given to individual Angels and Angelic Choirs, reflects some of the particular duties assigned to them, either in the Court of Heaven or on their missions to men here on earth. Such names are indicative of Angelic activity rather than of Angelic nature, but because operation is always in proportion to nature some aspect of the Angelic nature is revealed by such names, in a manner comprehensible to man. If they actually have proper names that fully express their nature, such names must be too wonderful for mortal man to understand. This is probably the reason why the Angel who appeared to Samson's mother, very carefully evaded her curious questioning in this regard. "A man of God came to me, having the countenance of an Angel, very awful. And when I asked him who he was, and whence he came, and by what name he was called, he would not tell me."[1] When the same Angel appeared to Samson's father, he too pressed the heavenly spirit for his name: "What is thy name, that, if thy word shall come to pass, we may honor thee. And he answered him: Why askest thou my name, which is wonderful?"[2]

[1] Judg. 13:6.
[2] *Ibid.* 17 f.

The patriarch Jacob had no more success with the Angel who wrestled with him: "Jacob asked him: Tell me by what name art thou called? He answered: Why dost thou ask my name? And he blessed him in the same place."[3] In both these instances the Angel does not deny the fact that he has a name, by which other Angels call him in heaven, but that name is too wonderful for man to hear. The name of a purely spiritual nature must be expressed by such exalted concepts as to be entirely ineffable in human terms. We believe that the danger of idolatry, which was very close in those days, was an added reason for the Angel not to give any name. The Holy Angels were always very careful in preventing man from offering sacrifices and divine worship to them. Manue, Samson's father, was about to make a sort of sacrificial offering to the Angel who had just spoken to him, when the Angel stopped him, saying: "If thou press me, I will not eat of thy bread, but if thou wilt offer a holocaust, offer it to the Lord."[4] Saint John the Evangelist was prevented from adoring an Angel: "And I, John, who have heard and seen these things. And, after I had heard and seen, I fell down to adore before the feet of the Angel who showed me these things, and he said to me: See thou do it not, for I am thy fellow servant, and of thy brethren the prophets, and of them that keep the words of the prophecy of this book. Adore God."[5] It is a very consoling thought to know that we are fellow servants of the Angels, if we serve God faithfully, like the prophets and the Apostles.

The Name eLOHIM

Because of the superior attributes of splendor, beauty, wisdom, and power manifested by the Angels on their various

[3] Gen. 32:29.
[4] Judg. 13:16.
[5] Apoc. 22:8 f.

apparitions to man, it was natural that at the very beginning of revelation, man would regard the Angels as divine beings. As a matter of fact, one of their names, in the Scriptures of the Old Testament, is Elohim, the very same name which was given to God, to Godlike beings, and to false gods. This name, in the sense of heavenly spirits, is found in several passages in the book of Psalms: "Let them be all confounded that adore graven things, and that glory in their idols. Adore Him, all you his Angels"[6] (*elohim*—the gods). Again, "I will sing praise to thee in the sight of the Angels"[7] (*elohim*—the gods). In these and similar passages the probable translation is, God, or gods, but from the context it appears that, more probably, Angels are meant here by *elohim*.[8] This is exactly how the Vulgate and other ancient versions, like the Septuagint, understood it. When the Angels are called gods, the word must be taken in a sense similar to that whereby saints and prophets are called gods: "I have said: You are gods, and all of you the sons of the most High."[9] Our Divine Savior fully approves this expression, in the sense of a just man and a saint being a partaker of the divine nature, adding that "the scripture cannot be broken."[10] The parallelism of the second stich: "and all of you the sons of the most High," clearly explains the meaning of the term "gods," in the first stich, namely, gods as adoptive sons of God; gods not by nature but by grace and adoption.

The Name "Sons of God" (BeNEY eLOHIM)

This name, like the preceding one, is applied to both Angels and just men. We have met this title before, at the very be-

[6] Ps. 96:7.
[7] Ps. 137:1.
[8] W. G. Heidt, *Angelology of the Old Testament*, p. 2 ff.
[9] Ps. 81:6.
[10] John 10:34 f.

ginning of this book, and we have discussed its meaning with reference to Angels. Because of the sanctifying grace which is in them, they are deified and children of God by adoption. This supernatural, divine element of sanctifying grace joins together Angels and just men into one family, God's family, making them all children of the same Father. The fellowship of grace and glory makes Angels and Saints *Sons of God,* and, therefore, brethren according to grace, if not according to nature.

The Name "Messenger" (MALeAKH)

This is the most common name given to all the heavenly spirits. The title is obviously taken from the most frequent and best known duty of the Angels, that of acting as God's messengers and legates to men. As explained before, this title is used both as a generic and a specific appelative; first, it refers to all the heavenly spirits of any rank or Choir, secondly, it is the proper name of the spirits of the last Choir in the last Hierarchy.

The Name "Mediators" (MELIS)

This and the following titles, common to all the Angels, are descriptive rather than nominal, and they are found only in the Scripture of the Old Testament. An example of this title is found in the book of Job: "If there shall be an Angel (a mediator) speaking for him, one among thousands, to declare man's uprightness."[11] The good Angels, especially our guardian Angels, are our mediators, those who speak for us before the divine throne of God. The Archangel Raphael was such a mediator for old Tobias, as it appears from his own words: "When thou didst pray with tears, and didst bury the dead, and didst leave thy dinner, and hide the dead by day in thy house, and bury

[11] Job 33:23.

them at night, I offered thy prayer to the Lord."[12] This offering of man's prayers and good deeds to the Lord is an act of mediation. Before the Savior's Ascension, before the gates of heaven were opened to redeemed mankind, the Holy Angels were man's only mediators and intercessors in Heaven. Their mediation did not cease after our Redemption by Christ, when the Queen of Heaven and all the Saints became our intercessors in union with Christ our Divine Mediator. On the contrary, the Angelic mediation became more incessant and efficacious because of the example of the Son of God. In the sacred liturgy of the Mass, the Church expresses this idea of Angelic mediation in the following beautiful prayer: "We humbly beseech Thee, Almighty God, bid these our offerings to be brought by the hands of Thy holy Angel unto Thy altar above, before the face of Thy divine majesty."[13] All this is in accordance with Saint John's apocalyptic vision: "Another Angel came, and stood before the altar, having a golden censer, and there was given to him much incense, that he should offer of the prayers of all the saints upon the golden altar, which is before the throne of God. And the smoke of the incense of the prayers of the saints ascended up before God from the hand of the Angel."[14] As mediators the Angels prove themselves to be man's most interested and sincere friends.

The Names "Ministers" (MeSARETH), and "Servants" ('EBHEdH)

Doing always the will of God and ministering to Him is the main duty of the Angels, hence one would expect that the Scripture occasionally call them Ministers and Servants of the Lord. This is the case especially in poetic books, as for example:

[12] Tob. 12:12.
[13] The Roman Missal: Canon: *Supplices te rogamus,* etc.
[14] Apoc. 8:3 f.

"Bless the Lord, all ye his hosts: you ministers of his that do his will."[15] "Behold in his servants he puts no trust, and in his Angels he finds folly."[16] According to the law of poetical parallelism, here the terms hosts and ministers, servants and Angels are synonyms. Under the aspect of ministers and servants the Angels offer a luminous example to man, and particularly to priests as ministers of the Church and dispensers of the mysteries of God. The priest, according to Saint Paul, is "a minister of the holies and of the true tabernacle, which the Lord hath pitched, and not man."[17]

The Name "Watcher" ('IR)

It is only in the book of *Daniel* that we meet this appellative for the Angels. The watcher is always called a holy one in these passages. "I saw in the vision of my head upon my bed: and behold a watcher and a holy one came down from heaven."[18] "And whereas the king saw a watcher and a holy one come down from heaven, and say: Cut down the tree and destroy it, but leave the stump of the roots thereof in the earth."[19] The name "watcher" is very appropriate, for the heavenly spirits never sleep or rest but are ever vigilant and ready to carry out God's commands while beholding the life-giving splendor of His glory.

The Name "Host" or "Army" (SABHA)

The term Host, as applied to Angels, is usually found in its plural form SeBHA'OTH, and in connection with the word

---

[15] Ps. 102:21.
[16] Job 4:18. This version is directly from the Hebrew.
[17] Heb. 8:2.
[18] Dan. 4:10.
[19] *Ibid.* 20.

heaven, as in the following passage: "I saw the Lord sitting on his throne, and all the army (host) of heaven standing by him on the right hand and on the left."[20] A direct parallelism between Angels and Hosts is manifest in the following verse: "Praise ye him, all his Angels: praise ye him, all his hosts."[21] In these and similar passages the terms Hosts, Army, do not necessarily give the idea of a warlike preparation for military strife, they rather imply a well-ordered and well-organized multitude of heavenly spirits, most powerful and ever ready to obey God, the King of heaven, the Lord of Hosts.

The Name "Holy" or "Holy Ones" (QADHOS)

The qualification of sanctity expressed by the name Holy is based upon the supernatural and blessed life of the Angels in heaven. Sanctified by the infusion of divine grace from the beginning of their creation, perfected in it by their individual cooperation and their perseverance during the period of their probation, the Holy Angels are now confirmed in grace and they enjoy the never-ending Beatific Vision of God. They are truly saints, sons of God, ministers of the Court of Heaven, members of God's household. They are the assembly of the saints whereof the inspired Psalmist sings: "The heavens shall confess thy wonders, O Lord, and thy truth in the assembly of the saints. . . . God who is glorified in the assembly of the saints, great and terrible above all them that are about him."[22] "The Lord my God shall come, and all the saints with him."[23] The prophet Daniel refers to Angels when in his vision he hears saints talking to one another: "And I heard one of the saints speaking, and

[20] II Par. 18:18.
[21] Ps. 148:2.
[22] Ps. 88:6, 8.
[23] Zach. 14:5.

one saint said to another, I know not to whom that was speaking."[24]

The infinite sanctity of God is revealed to His Angels in the glory of heaven; they almost breathe it, and they reflect it in themselves according to their capacity. That sanctity is reflected in all their apparitions to men here on earth.

---

[24] Dan. 8:13. Another name, common to all the Angels, is the word "spirit" (RUACH), especially in its plural form (Apoc. 1:4 and 4:5). But because the word applies more commonly to evil and unclean spirits, and to any breath of life and to winds, we do not regard it as clearly and exclusively referring to Angels.

Chapter V

THE NINE CHOIRS OF THE ANGELS

Specific Names of the Angels

IN the preceding chapter are explained the names common to all the Angels of heaven without distinction of Hierarchy or rank, and something about their nature by the simple analysis of those names. We know that the spirit world is divided in Hierarchies and Choirs, each Choir having its proper denomination which should reveal something that is characteristic of all the members of the same Choir. The names we have analyzed in the preceding chapter reveal something generic; here we have something more specific. Every Angel of the first Choir, in the first Hierarchy, is a Seraph; all together they are Seraphim. There is something in all of them that is not found in any other Angel of any other Choir or Hierarchy. What is this common element? This is what we intend to find out by analyzing the specific names of the Angelic Choirs.

Every Angelic Choir has its own specific unity, a unity based upon something common to all the Angels of that Choir that is not found in others. This constitutes the specific difference between Choir and Choir. This specific difference does not exclude other differences between the individual Angels pertaining to the same Choir. These would have to be regarded as individual differences between members of the same species, or better, quasi-species. We have already remarked once before that individual differences between Angels of the same Choir are themselves specific, because every Angel, according to Saint Thomas, differs from another Angel of the same rank according to form, and not according to matter or quantity; hence the individual difference is itself specific as every difference according to form must necessarily be. In order to distinguish between these two specific differences found in every Angel, we call the first *hierarchical*, the second *individual*. The hierarchical difference distinguishes the members of one choir from those of another, whereas the individual difference distinguishes between one Angel and another within the same Choir.

Following are the nine Choirs of Angels in their descending hierarchical order: *Seraphim, Cherubim, Thrones; Dominations, Virtues, Powers; Principalities, Archangels, Angels.*

1. The Seraphim

Seraphim, from the Hebrew *saraph:* to burn.

This is the first Choir of the supreme Hierarchy of the Angels. The name Seraphim is the plural form of the word; the singular is Seraph. This name occurs only twice in Sacred Scripture. It is found in chapter 6 of Isaias where they are described as standing upon the throne where the Lord was sitting, having each six wings, and singing constantly the hymn of glory: Holy, Holy, Holy. The description here given by the prophet, their very name, which means the *burning ones,* their position next to the throne of the Most High God, the act of purging the lips of the prophet with fire (a live coal taken from the altar) are all circumstances that in a sensible form reveal the exalted position of the Seraphim in the Court of heaven. "I saw the Lord sitting upon a throne high and elevated, and his train filled the temple. Upon it stood the seraphims: the one had six wings, and the other had six wings: with two they covered his face, with two they covered his feet, and with two they flew."[1]

[1] Isa. 6:1 f.

The meaning of burning ones, implied by the etymology of the name Seraphim, is to be understood in both the transitive and the intransitive sense of the verb. In his epistle to Pope Damasus, Saint Jerome notes that *Seraphim* translated from the Greek means *the inflaming ones,* or, *the burning ones.*[2] They are described as having each three pairs of wings with one of which they covered their face as a token of profound reverence and in order not to be seen, with another they covered their feet out of modesty and respect, with the third they flew. A general resemblance to a human figure seems to be implied, but it is not said what their face looked like. The love of God wherewith they glow keeps them close to the throne of the Divine Majesty, but their profound humility and reverence interpose the screen of their wings between themselves and the superbrilliant splendors of the Glory of the Most High.

The primary duty of the Seraphim is to sing without ceasing to God, celebrating above all the other attributes the Holiness of God, a perfection which characterizes all of God's attributes, for holy is His Justice, holy His Goodness, holy His Mercy, holy His Power, holy His Beauty, holy His Wisdom, etc. Hence the Seraphic hymn of glory heard by the Prophet was this: "Holy, holy, holy, the Lord God of hosts, all the earth is full of his glory."[3] The vehemence of their feelings and of their devotion appears from the fact that their song is such a powerful cry that "the lintels of the doors were moved at the voice of him that cried," namely the Seraphim who "cried one to another." The temple, where this vision appeared, was filled with smoke, a symbol perhaps of that fire of love of the Seraphim, "the Burning Ones."

Another duty is made manifest in this vision of Isaias by the action of one of the seraphim, namely the purging with fire:

[2] Epist. XVIII, ML 22:364.
[3] Isa. 6:3.

"One of the seraphims flew to me: and in his hand was a live coal, which he had taken with the tongs off the altar. And he touched my mouth, and said: Behold this hath touched thy lips, and thy iniquities shall be taken away, and thy sin shall be cleansed."[4]

From the notion of burning contained in their name, it was obvious to the popular mind to regard the Seraphim as the spirits of love. Seraphic, today, is said of a person whose life is completely ruled by divine love, such as the Seraphic Saint Francis of Assisi, the Seraphic Virgin of Avila, Saint Teresa, and Saint Catherine of Siena.

According to Dionysius, "the name Seraphim clearly indicates their ceaseless and eternal revolution about Divine Principles; their heat and their keenness, the exuberance of their intense, perpetual, tireless activity, and their elevative and energetic assimilation of those below, kindling them and firing them to their own heat, and wholly purifying them by a burning and all-consuming flame, and by the unhidden, unquenchable, changeless, radiant, and enlightening power, dispelling and destroying the shadows of darkness."[5]

2. The Cherubim

Cherubim, from the singular word KeRUBH.

Scholars differ widely on the meaning and the origin of this word. It seems that this was originally an Assyrian word which was later given a definite meaning by the Hebrews. Assyrians, Persians, and Egyptians paid great honor to protective deities, named in Accadian *Kuribu,* or *Karubu* (the probable origin of *Kerubh* and *Kerubhim*), represented as winged bulls, winged lions or sphinxes, with animal bodies and human faces of colossal proportions. These protective deities were the common guardians

[4] *Ibid.* 6.   [5] *The Cel. Hier.,* VII.

of temples and tombs, where some such statues can still be seen. Between these pagan deities and the Hebrew *Kerubh, Kerubhim,* there is nothing in common except perhaps the name, and a similarity of duties, but of a much higher order. In Sacred Scripture, the Cherubim appear as heavenly custodians and protectors of holy places and holy things. The Cherubim are the first among all the Angels to be mentioned in the Bible: "And the Lord God . . . placed before the paradise of pleasure cherubims, and a flaming sword, turning every way, to keep the way of the tree of life."[6] We find that the Lord commanded Moses to make images of two Cherubim in the Tabernacle, thereby representing them as guardians and protectors of holy places and of sacred things: "Thou shalt make also two cherubims of beaten gold, on the two sides of the oracle. Let one cherub be on the one side, and the other on the other. Let them cover both sides of the propitiatory, spreading their wings and covering the oracle: and let them look one towards the other, their faces being turned towards the propitiatory wherewith the ark is to be covered."[7] Here the Scripture offers a description of images of Cherubim in beaten gold, whereas in Genesis reference was made to the heavenly spirits themselves, the real Cherubim. In both passages they are represented as protective spirits and custodians of sacred things.

Another specific duty of the Cherubim seems to be that of being the throne-bearers of Almighty God. In speaking of God, the sacred writers often describe Him as sitting upon the Cherubim: "Thou that sittest upon the cherubims, shine forth."[8] Again, "The Lord hath reigned, let the people be angry; he that sitteth on the cherubims, let the earth be moved."[9] The

[6] Gen. 3:23 f.
[7] Exod. 25:18 ff.
[8] Ps. 79:2.
[9] Ps. 98:1.

prophet Isaias addresses our Lord by using three of the most common titles reserved for the Divinity: "O Lord of hosts, God of Israel, who sittest upon the cherubims."[10] David describes the Cherubim as the living chariot of God: "And he [God] ascended upon the cherubim, and he flew; he flew upon the wings of the winds."[11] Yet, it was centuries later that this idea of the Cherubim as a living chariot of Yahweh became more elaborate. The author of Ecclesiasticus tells us that "it was Ezechiel that saw the glorious vision, which was shown him upon the chariot of cherubims."[12] The entire chapter 10 of Ezechiel deals with this vision: "And I saw, and behold in the firmament that was over the heads of the cherubims, there appeared over them as it were the sapphire stone, as the appearance of the likeness of a throne. And he spoke to the man that was clothed with linen, and said: Go in between the wheels that are under the cherubims and fill thy hand with the coals of fire that are between the cherubims, and pour them out upon the city . . . And the sound of the wings of the cherubims was heard even to the outward court as the voice of God Almighty speaking . . . And there appeared in the cherubims the likeness of a man's hand under the wings. And I saw, and behold there were four wheels by the cherubims; one wheel by one cherub, and another wheel by another cherub, and the appearance of the wheels was to the sight like the chrysolite stone . . . And when the cherubims went, the wheels also went by them. And when the cherubims lifted their wings, to mount up from the earth, the wheels stayed not behind, but went with them. When they stood, these stood, and when they were lifted up, these were lifted up, for the spirit of life was in them. And the glory of the Lord went forth from the threshold of the temple and stood over the

[10] Isa. 37:16.
[11] Ps. 17:11.
[12] Ecclus. 49:10.

cherubims. . . . This is the living creature which I saw under the God of Israel by the river Chobar, and I understood that they were cherubims. Each one had four faces, and each one had four wings, and the likeness of a man's hand was under their wings."[13] A similar vision is reported in chapter 1 of Ezechiel where these "living creatures," the Cherubim, are described more in detail.

Just as the Seraphim are popularly regarded as the spirits of divine love, so are the Cherubim considered as the spirits of heavenly wisdom. Commenting on Ezechiel's tenth chapter, Saint Gregory the Great defines the Cherubim as "the plenitude of knowledge." "These sublime hosts," he writes, "are called so, Cherubim, because they are filled with a knowledge which is most perfect since they are allowed to behold the glory of God most closely." Even before the days of Saint Gregory, Dionysius had stressed the light of knowledge as characteristic of the Cherubim: "The name Cherubim denotes their power of knowing and beholding God, their receptivity to the most high gift of light, their contemplation of the beauty of the Divinity in its first manifestation. They are filled by participation in divine wisdom, and bounteously outpour to those below them from their own fountain of wisdom."[14]

3. The "Thrones"

Sacred Scripture does not offer any clue about the nature and the duties of this Angelic Choir, beyond the fact of revealing its name at the head of a partial list: "In him [the Word] were all things created in heaven and on earth, visible and invisible,

[13] Ezech. 10:1-21.
[14] *Op. cit.,* 7. "The Cherubim," writes St. John Chrysostom, "appeared on earth, yet, they are heavenly. And why do I say 'appeared'? nay rather they dwell on earth, as indeed in Paradise; but this is nothing, for they are heavenly." *Homil. on Hebr. XVI,* 23.

whether thrones or dominations, or principalities, or powers."[15] Being the lower Choir of the first and highest Hierarchy, the Thrones share with the Seraphim and the Cherubim the exalted dignity and glory of being closer to the throne of God than all the rest of the Angelic Choirs. They also participate in a most exalted nature, required by the performance of the most transcending duties that are characteristic of the first Hierarchy. Because of their nearness to God, the light of the divine mysteries is brought to them before the rest. Steadfastness seems to be the characteristic of the Thrones. "The name of the most glorious and most exalted Thrones denotes that which is exempt from and untainted by any base and earthly thing. . . . They have no part in what is low but dwell in fullest power, immovably and perfectly established in the Most High."[16]

4. The Dominations

In Saint Paul's passage quoted above, the Dominations are mentioned without a word of comment or explanation. According to Dionysius they occupy the first place in the second Angelic Hierarchy. "The name given to the holy Dominations means, I think, a certain unbounded elevation to that which is above, freedom from all that is terrestrial, and from all inward inclination to the bondage of discord, a liberal superiority to harsh tyranny, freedom from degrading servility and from what is low, because they are untouched by any inconsistency. They are true lords, perpetually aspiring to true lordship and to the source of all lordship. . . . They do not turn towards vain shadows, but wholly give themselves to that true authority, forever one with the Godlike source of lordship."[17]

[15] Col. 1:16.
[16] Dionysius, *op. cit.*
[17] *Ibid.*

5. The Virtues

Saint Peter mentions "Angels, Powers, and Virtues"[18] referring to good Angels. Saint Paul speaks of "all Principality, and Power, and Virtue, and Dominion,"[19] likewise in the sense of good spirits. Once, however, the same Apostle mentions Virtues in the sense of spiritual powers hostile to Christ, that is, fallen angels: "When he [Christ] shall have brought to nought all principality, and power, and virtue."[20] According to Dionysius, "the name of holy Virtues signifies a certain powerful and unshakable courage welling forth into all their Godlike energies . . . mounting upwards in fullness of power to an assimilation with God, never falling away from the divine life through its own weakness, but ascending unwaveringly to the superessential Virtue which is the source of all virtue, fashioning itself as far as it may in virtue . . . and flowing forth providentially to those below it, filling them abundantly with virtue."[21]

6. The Powers

The holy Powers form the third and last Choir of the second Angelic Hierarchy. The name of this Choir is found occasionally also in the Scripture of the Old Testament, as in *Daniel*, "O all ye powers of the Lord, bless the Lord."[22] In the New Testament the name takes on the more specific meaning of a particular order of heavenly spirits, both good Angels and evil spirits. Good Angels are meant in the following passage: "That the manifold wisdom of God may be made known to the principalities and *powers* in heavenly places through the church."[23] Fallen angels, on the contrary, are meant here: "Our wrestling is not against flesh and blood, but against principalities and

18 I Pet. 3:22.
19 Eph. 1:21.
20 I Cor. 15:24.

21 *Op. cit.*
22 Dan. 3:61.
23 Eph. 3:10.

powers, against the rulers of the world of this darkness."[24] The nature of these heavenly spirits is thus described by Dionysius: "The name of the Holy Powers, co-equal with the divine Dominations and Virtues, signifies an orderly and unconfined order in the divine receptions, and the regulation of intellectual and supernatural power which never debases its authority by tyrannical force but is irresistibly urged on in due order to the divine. It beneficently leads those below it, as far as possible to the Supreme Power which is the source of power."[25]

7. The Principalities

The name of this Choir, like those of the two preceding ones, occurs both in the sense of good Angels and of demons. Speaking of the fallen angels, the Apostle Saint Jude singles out the Principalities as most representative of the Angelic Choirs in which defection occurred: "The angels who kept not their principality, but forsook their own habitation, he hath reserved under darkness, in everlasting chains, unto the judgment of the great day."[26] The term "principality" in the above passage might well be understood as that superior position of power and honor that was shared by all the Angels before their fall; yet, the constant association of Principalities with fallen angels, seems to offer sufficient ground to believe that this passage refers to them in a particular manner if not indeed exclusively.

Principalities are the first and leading Choir of the third and last Hierarchy of Angels. Their duties are thus described by Dionysius: "The name of celestial Principalities signifies their Godlike princeliness and authoritativeness in an order which is holy and most fitting to the princely powers, and that they are wholly turned towards the Prince of princes, and lead others in

[24] Eph. 6:12.
[25] *Op. cit.*
[26] Jude 1:6.

princely fashion. They are formed, as far as creatures can, in the likeness of the Source of principality and reveal Its transcendent order by the good order of the princely powers."[27]

8. The Archangels

The middle Choir of the third Hierarchy is perhaps the best known of all—with the exception of the Choir of Angels themselves—because of the missions and activities of three Archangels, as we shall report in the following chapter. From what is said there of the power, wisdom, and holiness of Saint Michael, Saint Gabriel, and Saint Raphael one may well realize what a glorious family God has in heaven, where millions upon millions of such superior beings minister unto Him. "The Choir of the Holy Archangels is placed in the same threefold order as the celestial Principalities. . . . Since each Hierarchy has first, middle, and last ranks, the holy order of Archangels, through its middle position, participates in the two extremes, being joined with the most holy Prnicipalities and with the holy Angels."[28] The name itself implies that Archangels are leaders among the Angels and superior to the Choir of Angels.

9. The Angels

Taken in the specific sense of a particular Choir, the Angels "fill up and complete the lowest Choir of all the Hierarchies of the celestial Intelligences, since they are the last of the heavenly beings possessing angelic nature. And they, indeed, are more properly named Angels (i.e., messengers) by us than are those of a higher rank, because their Choir is more directly in contact with visible and earthly things."[29]

[27] *Op. cit.,* 9.
[28] *Ibid.*
[29] *Ibid.*

By their nature and duties, the Angels are closer to man than any other celestial spirit. When the Psalmist says that God made man "a little less than the Angels,"[30] he was probably referring to these holy spirits of the last Choir, the closest link between the spirit world and rational man. It is from the ranks of this Choir that Guardian Angels are ordinarily, yet not exclusively, taken for the guidance and protection of individual souls during this earthly pilgrimage, as we shall explain later.

[30] Ps. 8:6.

Chapter VI

PROPER NAMES OF THE ANGELS

The Three Archangels

THE Sacred Scriptures have revealed the proper names of only three Angels, all of whom belong to the Choir of the Archangels. The names are well known to all, namely: Michael, Gabriel, Raphael. Ancient apocryphal literature of the Old Testament contains several other names of Archangels in addition to the three just mentioned. Like the sources themselves, these other names are spurious. Names like Uriel, Raguel, Sariel, and Jeremiel are not found in the canonical books of Sacred Scripture, but in the apocryphal book of Enoch, fourth book of Esdras,[1] and in rabbinical literature. The Church does not permit proper names of Angels that are not found in the canonical books of the Bible. All such names that were taken from apocryphal writings were rejected under Pope Zachary, in 745. There must have been danger of serious abuses in this regard during that century, because a similar step was taken in a synod held at Aix-la-Chapelle in 789.

The Archangel Michael

Michael from the Hebrew *Mikha'el,* meaning: *Who is as God?* His name is a battle cry; both shield and weapon in the

[1] IV Esd. 4:1.

struggle, and an eternal trophy of victory. The popularity of this name in the Old Testament appears from the fact that no less than ten persons bearing the name of Michael are mentioned in the sacred books, like: "Sthur the son of Michael."[2] A similar name is found also in the Accadian language with a meaning identical to that of Michael; the Accadian equivalent is *Mannu-ki-ili*.

As the proper name of one of the great Archangels, the word Michael appears for the first time in the book of the prophet Daniel, where he is called: "Michael, one of the chief princes,"[3] and again: "At that time shall Michael rise up, the great prince, who standeth for the children of thy people."[4]

The name "Archangel" is given only to Saint Michael, even though sacred tradition and the liturgy of the Church attribute the same title to Saint Gabriel and Saint Raphael: "When Michael, the archangel, disputing with the devil, contended about the body of Moses, he durst not bring against him the judgment of railing speech, but said: The Lord command thee."[5] In spite of such an explicit testimony of the Scripture, a few writers have maintained that Saint Michael, because of his exalted position among the Angels, must belong to a much higher order, perhaps to that of the Seraphim, rather than to the order of Archangels. We do not believe that this opinion can be defended. The exalted position occupied by Saint Michael can be explained by the fact that, even though he belongs to a relatively low order by nature, his outstanding zeal for the glory of God and the salvation of his fellow Angels, at the time of Satan's rebellion, merited him such glory and power as to equal and even to excel through grace such celestial spirits that belong to a

[2] Num. 13:14. *See also* I Par. 5:13, 14; 6:40; 7:3; 8:16; 12:20; II Par. 21:2; I Esdr. 8:8.

[3] Dan. 10:13.

[4] Dan. 12:1.

[5] Jude 1:9.

much higher Choir by nature. If we remember, the Angels lived through a period of probation during which they could merit each according to his works. The great variety of merit explains, in addition to other natural elements, the great difference in their glory and in their power.

Father Joseph Husslein points out that the Church calls Saint Michael "Prince of the heavenly hosts"—*Princeps militiae caelestis,* adding further: "The fact that the three Angels I have just mentioned are spoken of as Archangels need not imply more than that they were entrusted with extraordinary missions. Michael is the only one to whom the Scriptures apply this title, but there is good reason for the opinion that he may be the very highest of all the angels."[6] Saint Michael is indeed a prince of the heavenly hosts, but this is sufficiently explained by the power granted him by God and not necessarily by superiority of nature. We believe that a power of that sort would not be conferred upon Seraphim and Cherubim who are the living throne of God, but rather upon those who belong to the order of ministering spirits, namely Principalities, Archangels, and Angels, who "are sent to minister for them, who shall receive the inheritance of salvation."[7]

According to Gustav F. Oehler, "this name: Michael—Who is as God?—of the prince of the Angels does not imply merely a humble acknowledgement on the part of the Angel, but it is rather an actual assertion concerning the Angel himself. The name thus expresses the irresistibility of him to whom God gives the power to execute His behests."[8]

Saint Michael has always been the warrior Angel, fighting first Satan and his demons from the beginning, then, in the course of time, all the enemies of God's own people. He is "the great

---

[6] *The Spirit World About Us,* p. 117.

[7] Hebr. 1:14.

[8] *Theology of the Old Testament,* p. 446.

prince, who standeth for the children of thy people." As of old, so today, Saint Michael is the great defender of the Church of Christ on earth.

The now famous problem, "The Angel of the Lord," *Malakh Yahweh,* that has engaged the attention of Scripture scholars for decades, may perhaps be solved by admitting that this mysterious Angel of the Lord (who in various books of the Old Testament is represented as acting in the name of God Himself, and is often received and honored as God would), is none other than the Archangel Saint Michael, God's own legate to His people. The words of the prophet Daniel seem to insinuate this: "None is my helper in all these things, but Michael your prince."[9] "At that time shall Michael rise up, the great prince, who standeth for the children of thy people."[10] A legate can speak and act in the name and by the authority of the supreme ruler who sent him and whom he represents. This seems to have been Saint Michael's position with the children of Israel; he was both the heavenly Prince representing the King of Heaven and the heavenly protector of God's own people against both human and diabolical enemies.

Saint Michael who had defended and protected God's children in the spirit world, was to extend the same protection to the human children of God here on earth. Surrounded and threatened as they were by hostile pagan nations, over which Satan had established his tyrannical rule, Saint Michael could not remain indifferent to this new form of seduction and rebellion introduced by his archenemy among the children of men. As long as Satan persists in his attacks, the heavenly champion, the Prince of the heavenly hosts will continue to shatter his plans with the war cry of old: "Who is as God?" In the Old Testament, therefore, Saint Michael is the Angel par excellence, the Angel of the Lord, the national Guardian Angel of the Israelites.

[9] Dan. 10:21.   [10] Dan. 12:1.

At times, especially in the book of Exodus, this "Angel of the Lord" is called simply, the Lord; as for example in this passage, "And the Lord went before them to show the way by day in a pillar of a cloud, and by night in a pillar of fire, that he might be the guide of their journey at both times."[11] He who is called "the Lord" in this passage, is mentioned again in the same capacity as the "Angel of God" in the following passage: "And the Angel of God, who went before the camp of Israel, leaving the forepart, stood behind, between the Egyptian camp and the camp of Israel, and it was a dark cloud, and enlightening the night."[12] This very clever military maneuver clearly shows the strategy of the Prince of heavenly hosts.

As the national Guardian Angel of the Israelites, and God's special legate to His people, Saint Michael is introduced with words which reveal the great divine love and solicitude of the Lord, together with man's duties towards Guardian Angels in general: "Behold I will send my Angel who shall go before thee, and keep thee in thy journey, and bring thee into the place that I have prepared. Take notice of him, and hear his voice, and do not think him one to be contemned, for he will not forgive when thou hast sinned, and my name is in him. But if thou wilt hear his voice, and do all that I speak, I will be an enemy to thy enemies, and will afflict them that afflict thee."[13]

The other opinion which holds that the expression the "Angel of the Lord" is not really an Angel, or Saint Michael, but the Word of God (the Logos) God Himself, is now regarded as a mere conjecture and a rather obsolete opinion.[14]

Several apparitions of the Archangel Michael have been re-

---

[11] Exod. 13:21.
[12] Exod. 14:19 f.
[13] Exod. 23:20-22.
[14] W. G. Heidt, *Angelology of the Old Testament,* p. 96 f.

ported during the Christian centuries. One of the most outstanding of all such apparitions is the one which is commemorated in the universal Church on May 8. The Archangel Saint Michael appeared on Mount Gargano in Apulia, South Italy, in the days of Pope Gelasius (492-496). A shrine was erected in the cave of the apparition and it became the goal of devout pilgrimages in subsequent centuries. Another feast in honor of Saint Michael the Archangel, on September 29, formerly known as *Michaelmas,* is the anniversary of the Dedication of the former basilica of Saint Michael and all the Angels on the Salarian Way in Rome. An apparition, similar to that of Mount Gargano, was honored in the great shrine called *Michaelion,* near Constantinople, according to the historian Sozomenus, who wrote about the middle of the fifth century, a century of great devotion to the Holy Angels in general and to Saint Michael in particular.[15]

In the liturgy of the Mass Saint Michael is regarded as the Angel who leads the souls of the faithful departed to heaven: "Deliver them from the lion's mouth, that hell engulf them not, that they fall not into darkness; but let Michael, the holy standard-bearer, bring them into the holy light."[16]

Saint Michael is invoked in a particular manner in the prayers recited at the foot of the altar after Mass: "Saint Michael the Archangel, defend us in battle, etc." This particular prayer is a condensed form of the general exorcism against Satan and all the evil spirits, published by Pope Leo XIII.

As long as God's children are exposed to the attacks of Satan in this world, Saint Michael's battle cry: "Who is like God?" will continue to scare and shatter all the forces of evil, and his powerful intervention in the struggle in behalf of the children of God will never cease.

---

[15] *Ecclesiastical History,* Book II, Ch. III.
[16] The Mass for the Dead, Offertory.

The Archangel Gabriel

The name Gabriel seems to be composed of the Hebrew words, *gebher:* man, and *'el:* God. It means, therefore, *Man of God,* or, *Strength of God.*

Practically all the missions and manifestations of this Archangel are closely connected with the coming of the Messias.[17] The most accurate prophecy regarding the time of the coming of Christ was made by Saint Gabriel through the prophet Daniel.[18]

Immediately before the coming of Christ we meet the Archangel Gabriel in the temple of Jerusalem, announcing to Zachary the birth of a son, John the Baptist, the precursor of Christ: "I am Gabriel, who stand before God, and am sent to speak to thee, and to bring thee these good tidings."[19]

The greatest and by far the most joyful message ever committed to an Angel from the beginning of time, was the one brought by the Archangel Gabriel to the Virgin Mary, announcing to her the Incarnation of the Word of God and the birth of Christ, the Savior of mankind. The simplicity and heavenly grandeur of this message, as related to us by her who was the only witness to Gabriel's good tidings, should be read in full in order to understand the sublime and delicate mission of Gabriel in the work of human redemption.

It is the first time that a prince of the court of heaven greets an earthly child of God, a young woman, with a deference and respect a prince would show to his Queen. That Angel's flight to the earth marked the dawn of a new day, the beginning of a new covenant, the fulfillment of God's promises to His people: "The Angel Gabriel was sent from God into a city of Galilee, called Nazareth, to a virgin espoused to a man, whose name was

[17] Dan. 8:16 ff; 9:21 ff.
[18] *Ibid*. 26.
[19] Luke 1:19 f.

Joseph, of the house of David, and the virgin's name was Mary."[20]

Heavenly wisdom, tact, adroitness are evident in Gabriel's conversation with the Virgin Mary: "The Angel being come in said unto her: Hail, full of grace, the Lord is with thee."[21] Gabriel must overcome Mary's reaction of surprise at both his appearance and especially at his "manner of salutation." He has to prepare and dispose her pure virginal mind to the idea of maternity, and obtain her consent to become the mother of the Son of God. Gabriel nobly fulfills this task: "Fear not, Mary, for thou hast found grace with God." He calls her by her own name in order to inspire confidence and to show affection and solicitude in her perturbation. The great message is presented to her as a decree of the Most High God, a thing ordained in the eternal decree of the Incarnation, predicted centuries before by the prophets, and announced now to her as an event of imminent occurrence depending on her consent: "Behold thou shalt conceive in thy womb, and shalt bring forth a son, and thou shalt call his name Jesus. He shall be great, and shall be called the Son of the Most High; and the Lord God shall give unto him the throne of David his father and he shall reign in the house of Jacob for ever. And of his kingdom there shall be no end."[22] From these words of the Angel, it became very evident to Mary that her son was to be the promised Messias, the Son of David. But she did not know how to reconcile her vow of virginity with the promised motherhood, hence her question: "How shall this be done, because I know not man." Gabriel's reply shows that God wanted to respect Mary's vow of virginity and thus

[20] *Ibid.* 26 f.

[21] *Ibid.* 28. The Vulgate adds: "Blessed art thou among women," but this part of the greeting was probably added later, taking it from the words of St. Elizabeth, Luke 1:42. The Greek text has only the part given above.

[22] *Ibid.* 31-33.

make her a mother without a human father, in a unique and miraculous way: "The Holy Ghost shall come upon thee, and the power of the Most High shall overshadow thee."[23]

As a last word of encouragement and, at the same time, a most gratifying information, the Archangel reveals to Mary that her elderly and barren cousin Elizabeth is now an expectant mother in her sixth month of pregnancy. This final argument was offered in order "to prove that nothing can be impossible with God."[24]

Mary, unshaken in her profound humility, replied: "Behold the handmaid of the Lord; be it done to me according to thy word."[25] This reply was Mary's consent, a consent awaited by heaven and earth. The Archangel Gabriel departed from Mary to bring to all the Angels the glorious tidings of the Incarnation of the Word.

It seems very probable that Gabriel, the Archangel of the Annunciation, was given special charge of the Holy Family of Nazareth. He was probably the Angel who brought "good tidings of great joy" to the shepherds "keeping night watches over their flock," the night that Christ was born of the Virgin Mary in Bethlehem. We notice, on this occasion, the same procedure of first assuaging fear and surprise, as had been the case at Mary's Annunciation by Gabriel: "Fear not, for, behold, I bring you good tidings of great joy. . . . This day is born to you a Savior, who is Christ the Lord, in the city of David." Who else could be the messenger of such good tidings, but he who had promised them through the prophet Daniel, and announced them to Mary, Gabriel the Archangel?

Having delivered the joyful message, the Archangel is joined suddenly by a vast multitude of the heavenly hosts, singing for

[23] *Ibid.* 35.
[24] *Ibid.* 36.
[25] *Ibid.* 38.

the first time in this valley of tears the canticle of the celestial Sion. It was fitting that the Archangel of Redemption should intone the canticle of human redemption: "Suddenly there was with the Angel a multitude of the heavenly army, praising God, and saying: Glory to God in the highest, and on earth peace to men of good will."[26]

Gabriel's duties towards the Messias did not come to an end with his birth. Gabriel was probably the Angel who "appeared in sleep to Joseph," first in Bethlehem when he warned him saying: "Arise, and take the child and his mother, and flee into Egypt, and be there until I shall tell you. For it will come to pass that Herod will seek the child to destroy him."[27] After the death of Herod the Angel appeared to Joseph again in Egypt to tell him to bring the child and his mother back into the land of Israel.

Gabriel who is "the strength of God" must have been the Angel mentioned by Saint Luke, in his narrative of Christ's agony in the garden: "And there appeared to him an Angel from heaven, strengthening him."[28] It was fitting that the Angel who had witnessed the Savior's agony, and who had announced His coming to both the Old and New Testament, should also be the first to announce to the world the Savior's Resurrection, His triumph over sin and death on Easter morning: "An Angel of the Lord descended from heaven, and coming rolled back the stone, and sat upon it. And his countenance was as lightning, and his raiment as snow."[29]

It is very probable that the Archangel Gabriel is meant when Saint Paul speaks of the second coming of Christ at the end of the world, when Saint Michael's struggle with Satan shall be over, and when all the physical and spiritual remedies of Saint Raphael are needed no more. It would seem that of the three

[26] *Ibid.* 2:12 ff.
[27] Matt. 2:13.
[28] Luke 22:43.
[29] Matt. 28:2.

Archangels known to us, Saint Gabriel is the one who with a mighty voice will call the dead to life and to judgment:' "The Lord himself shall come down from heaven with commandment, and with the voice of an archangel, and with the trumpet of God; and the dead who are in Christ shall rise first."[30] The voice of the Archangel and the trumpet of God seem to be the same thing, having the purpose to convey the divine command to the dead to rise again by the power of the Almighty God. The resurrection of "the dead who are in Christ" is the harvest, the gathering of the fruits of Redemption. Gabriel, who helped along during the long day of man's life on earth, in preparing man for the work of Redemption by the Messias, would seem to be the first among the Angels who are sent out to gather the elect from the four corners of the earth.

The Archangel Raphael

Raphael, from the Hebrew *rapha':* to heal, and *'el:* God, means "God heals," or the "Divine healer."

The history of Tobias, father and son, contains the grandest angelophany of the whole Bible, and it all revolves around the manifestation of the Archangel Raphael under the assumed name and form of a beautiful young man named Azarias. At the very end of his long mission the Archangel revealed his own identity and his real name, together with the actual purpose of his mission: "And now the Lord hath sent me to heal thee, and to deliver Sara thy son's wife from the devil. For I am the angel Raphael, one of the seven, who stand before the Lord."[31] In this angelophany, Saint Raphael reveals himself as a divine healer not only of physical infirmities, the blindness of old

[30] I Thess. 4:15.
[31] Tob. 12:14 f. All scriptural quotations concerning the two Tobias' reported in the following pages are from the book of Tobias.

Tobias, but also of spiritual afflictions and diabolical vexations, as in the case of Sara, young Tobias' wife. Had not the Archangel resorted to an assumed human form and personality, it might not have been possible for him to consort in such a familiar way with men, for several consecutive weeks, because of the instinctive fear that man experiences in the presence of celestial beings. Had either father or son, or both, known the real identity of the stranger, from the beginning, the Angelic mission could not have been accomplished in the charming human way in which it was actually carried out. However, the assumed form, and especially the assumed name and paternity—"Azarias the son of the great Ananias"—has been regarded by some as a sort of deception and a lie. However, the perfect sanctity of the Angels is opposed to even the appearance of sin and deception, even to what we call a white lie. In order to carry out his mission, it was necessary for the Angel to assume a form perceptible to man, a human form and a human name. In this case he assumed the appearance of an Israelite, a young relative of Tobias himself. By divine command the Archangel was to act as proxy for that young Israelite, Azarias, whose name he took; hence there was no lie on his part when he gave the name of the person he was representing in his human form. His true identity was revealed at the close of his mission, and whatever misconception had been created in the minds of the various persons he had met, was completely removed, and these were then grateful to the Archangel not only for his many benefits but also for his consideration in dealing with them like a human being. Besides, the Archangel was not hiding a human name and personality and giving another instead; in taking the place of Azarias he could in all truth call himself Azarias.

The story of the Archangel Raphael and the two Tobias' is too beautiful and too instructive for us to dismiss it with a simple reference: it reveals how Angels act when in human form; their Angelic nature, their power, wisdom, holiness are made manifest in the various incidents of this charming narrative. The Archangel is God's legate, he carries out God's plan acting as an instrument of Divine Providence, and Divine Goodness.

The old, charitable, and pious man Tobias is blind and feels that his days are numbered. He gives his young son Tobias some godly admonitions and tells him of some money he had lent to Gabelus of the city of Rages in Media, many years back, for which he had a regular note with Gabelus' signature. He wants his son to go and collect that money, but he first wants him to find a man to accompany him on the long journey: "Go now and seek thee out some faithful man, to go with thee for his hire, that thou may receive it, while I yet live."

While this was going on in Tobias' home, Heaven was listening in and preparing the companion, the "faithful man" young Tobias was looking for. The Lord gave the Archangel Raphael the command to appear as a young man named Azarias, to accompany young Tobias to the land of the Medes, and to bring peace and happiness to two God-fearing but very unhappy families. As the young man stepped out of his house in search of a companion, one morning, the Archangel Raphael was there as if waiting for him, in the disguise of "a beautiful young man." "And not knowing that he was an Angel of God, he saluted him, and said: From whence art thou, good young man? But he answered: Of the children of Israel." In a very short time the Archangel informed young Tobias that he knew the road to Gabelus, and knew Gabelus himself, having spent some time there; he knew all that country very well. Tobias could hardly believe in such a happy coincidence. Immediately he took his new friend and companion and returned to his blind father. The Angel who well knew the purpose of his mission, implicitly announced it in his words of greeting directed to the blind old man, when he said: "Joy be to thee always!"

Not knowing who was he who wished him joy, old Tobias replied: "What manner of joy shall be to me, who sit in darkness, and see not the light of heaven." Here the Archangel Raphael became more explicit, making both a promise and a prophecy: "Be of good courage, thy cure from God [God heals, was Raphael's own name] is at hand." He could not say more without engendering suspicion and betraying his own identity. Old Tobias regarded those kind words as an expression of good will and paid no particular attention to them; he had heard such expressions so often in the past. His interest is now in the voyage of his son, and he wants to know in whose hands he is committing the life of his only child and part of his own fortune. Upon hearing that the young guide is no less than Azarias, the son of the great Ananias, he remarks: "Thou art of a great family." Old Tobias, like his kinsman Gabelus, later on in this story, expresses his belief in the protection and guidance of guardian Angels. Not knowing that an Archangel is actually accompanying his son, he says: "May you have a good journey, and God be with you on your way, and his Angel accompany you." Had this circumstance been known to him, both he and his wife would have been spared all the worry and the sleepless nights during the long absence of their son. One thought, however, sustained the mind of old Tobias during his waiting: "Our son is safe: that man with whom we sent him is very trustworthy."

How carefree, and how joyful must have been that journey for young Tobias. To travel in the happy company of an Angel! He knew the road so well. He was never in doubt about anybody or anything they met on the road; always cheerful, never tired or sleepy; so sweet and kind in his conversation, yet always full of respect and attention. He was deeply spiritual and profoundly devout in his prayers, pure in all his words and actions. How true and inspired were the words of old Tobias when, comforting his weeping wife, he said to her: "I believe that the good Angel of God doth accompany him, and doth order all things well that are about him, so that he shall return to us with joy."

The sacred text remarks that when young Tobias started on his journey with his Angel companion, his pet dog followed him all the way to the East. Tobias was one of the thousands of Israelites living in the Babylonian captivity. Some of them had settled down in neighboring provinces, such as Mesopotamia, Assyria, and Media. It was exactly in this last province of Media that Tobias' kinsman Raguel lived with his family. This was not really the goal of his trip to the East, but it was here that God and His Angel wanted him to go; whereas his father had sent him to collect his money from Gabelus in the city of Rages in the mountains of Ecbatana, in Media. The Angel by diverting his trip accomplished more fully his mission, bringing unexpected joy and happiness to three families.

Having left his home town, the great city of Ninive, that morning, Tobias and his guide reached the river Tigris just before dark. They decided to spend that night by the bank of the Tigris. Here the Archangel Raphael began to reveal medical knowledge and experience. At the same time he provided food for that evening and for the rest of the journey. Weary of walking all day, young Tobias went to wash his feet in the cool water of the river before retiring. Here the sight of a monstrous fish that seemed to be coming up to devour him, frightened him exceedingly and made him cry for help: "Sir, he cometh upon me!" The Angelic guide, without coming to his rescue, instructed him on what to do, both giving him directions and inspiring him with confidence. At the end of the first day young Tobias had not yet acquired familiarity with his guide, so he calls him, Sir. Later he will call him brother. When the monstrous fish had been successfully drawn out of the river,

it was cut open, roasted, and salted. "Take out the entrails of this
fish," ordered the Angel, "and lay up his heart, and his gall, and
his liver for thee, for these are necessary for useful medicines."
These, no doubt, may have seemed strange medicines to young
Tobias and he wanted to know when and how to use them.
Here he begins to show more confidence and affection for the
heavenly guide: "I beseech thee, brother Azarias, tell me what
remedies are these things good for, which thou hast bid me keep
of the fish." The Angel explains the medical virtue of those
parts of the fish. More practical details are imparted as the
proper time for their use approaches. The liver of the fish was
needed as a material ingredient for an exorcism in order to
free Tobias' future wife Sara from the evil influence of the
devil; the gall was to be used for the cure of the blindness of
old Tobias.

The Archangel Raphael had been sent by God to cure and
comfort two afflicted souls, old Tobias and Raguel's young
daughter Sara, the widow of seven husbands, all of whom had
died on the first night following their wedding to her.

As night was falling, at the end of another day of their long
journey, young Tobias turning to his guide asked him the
customary question: "Where wilt thou that we lodge?" Here begins the first part of Raphael's mission. He must induce young
Tobias to marry Sara, Raguel's daughter, and at the same time
deliver her from all diabolical influence and vexation. This
was a very delicate matter, for sinister rumors about this young
dame, as being the cause of death to seven husbands, had reached
Ninive and young Tobias himself knew all about her and was
deathly afraid of associating with her. At the question of where
to lodge for the night, Raphael had proposed to put up at
Raguel's and for Tobias to propose to Sara, his own cousin.
"I hear," answered Tobias, "that she hath been given to seven
husbands, and they all died; moreover I have heard, that a

devil killed them." Imagine this young man, now, going to ask for the hand of such a dame! The Archangel Raphael obtained just that, and what is more, their marriage was a very happy one, blessed with good health and long life, so that they both saw their children's children to the fifth generation. The instructions on marital union given by the Archangel Raphael to young Tobias on this occasion remain an ideal of moral perfection for married couples for all time. Prayer, continence, and pure intention dispose the soul for God's blessings and thwart all influence of the evil spirit. Young Tobias listened intently to his heavenly guide and later carried out his instructions most faithfully, first repeating them to his bride: "We are the children of the saints, and we must not be joined together like heathens that know not God."

Amid the charming and intimate family reunion in Raguel's home, described in chapter seven of the book of Tobias, an unseen struggle goes on in the spirit world. Young Azarias (the Archangel Raphael) absents himself for a very short while from the gathering of the family and friends in order to attend to a very important business of his own. During those few minutes, Raphael, in the name and with the power of God, "took the devil, and bound him in the desert of upper Egypt." This devil Asmodeus, who had caused so much sorrow to Sara and her family, was Satan himself. With the exile of the spirit of evil, joy, peace and all blessings came to Raguel's home. Having attended to his business, young Azarias returned and took his place at the wedding feast, while actually contemplating the face of the Father Who is in heaven. The following morning, leaving Tobias there with his happy bride, he continues on the journey, accompanied by four servants and two camels. He finally found Gabelus and collected the money for old Tobias and, on his return, he took Gabelus to the wedding feast of his kinsman young Tobias.

The last part of the mission entrusted to Raphael the Archangel was now to follow. Having brought joy and happiness to Sara and all her family, it was time to bring a similar and even greater joy to old Tobias and his wife. The slow pace of the caravan that accompanied the bride to Ninive did not suit the Archangel who well knew the pain and the worries of Tobias' old parents: "Brother Tobias," said the Archangel, thou knowest how thou didst leave thy father. If it please thee, let us go before, and let the family follow softly after us, together with thy wife and with the beasts." Tobias agreed and taking with himself the gall of the fish, he and the Angel began to advance with much greater speed, the dog following them. It was time now to give the final instruction as to the use of the gall: "As soon as thou shalt come into the house, forthwith adore the Lord thy God, and giving thanks to Him, go to thy father and kiss him, and immediately anoint his eyes with this gall of the fish. . . . Thy father shall see the light of heaven, and shall rejoice in the sight of thee."

In the meantime Tobias' old mother was waiting for her son, sitting daily on top of a hill, scanning the horizon for a sign of her son and his guide. Finally one day Tobias' pet dog, running ahead brought the joyful news to the afflicted parents by his fawning and wagging his tail. All these human and earthly elements blend beautifully with the heavenly in this charming story of Angels and men.

Everything happened as promised by the Angel. Old Tobias regained his sight. At this point the heart of young Tobias was filled with gratitude, love, and admiration for his wonderful guide; so many and so great were the benefits received through him. Having witnessed the miraculous cure of his father he could find no words to express his feelings: "We are filled with all good things through him," he kept telling his father. Old Tobias understood that it was God Who was actually working all these marvels through young Azarias, and thus, full of reverence, he calls the young guide a holy man: "What can we give to this holy man, that is come with thee?"

The Lord never permits man to remain in error because of the disguise assumed by His ministering spirits in any of their apparitions. Sooner or later the truth about them will be made manifest. For several weeks in succession, the Archangel Raphael had been acting under assumed human form and human name. Now that his mission has been happily completed, he begins to prepare his two friends, father and son, for a great surprise, the revelation of his real self. At the moment that they both humbly approach him offering one half of everything that had been brought home as payment for his service, young "Azarias" answers with a wonderful explanation of why God has so blessed them. He recalls to the mind of old Tobias all the good he did in his days, his charity, his mercy, his patience, his alms, and his tearful prayers. Thus he begins to reveal himself gradually in order not to frighten them with a sudden disclosure. The enumeration of all the good deeds and of secrets of conscience known only to God are the first step in this revelation; the second is the statement: "Now the Lord hath sent me to heal thee, and to deliver Sara thy son's wife from the devil." The third and final step was liable to trouble and frighten them, hence he begins with comforting and reassuring words: "Peace be to you; fear not." As he said this, both father and son fell upon the ground on their faces, for suddenly the human form of Azarias was transfigured into that of an Archangel of light and beauty, and the final revelation came: "I am the Angel Raphael, one of the seven, who stand before the Lord . . . when I was with you I was there by the will of God: bless ye him, and sing praises to him." This is the only reward that he will accept, but none of the material things, money and cattle and clothes offered him generously by his good friends. Yet, these could still entertain some doubts, because they had seen him eat and drink like any other human being, and Angels do not eat and drink as men do. To this secret doubt he answers with saying: "I seemed indeed to eat and to drink with you, but I use an invisible meat and drink, which cannot be seen by men." Now that his work has been done, and that they know that God has sent His Angel to fill them with blessings, it is time for him to return to Heaven: "It is time therefore that I return to him that sent me; but bless ye God, and publish all his wonderful works." Here the Archangel returned to his invisible form, and from the company of men returned to that of the Angels.

Raphael, the Divine healer, seems to have been at work at Jerusalem, in the days of Christ our Lord, in the pool called Bethsaida by the Sheepgate. In the five porticoes surrounding that pool there was a multitude of sick people, waiting for the action of the Angel upon the water of the pool, an action which cured immediately any person who first descended into the pool: "An Angel of the Lord used to come down at certain times into the pool and the water was moved. And he that went down first into the pool after the motion of the water, was cured of whatever infirmity he had."[32]

The health-giving ministry of Saint Raphael may still be seen in the miraculous cures that have taken place up to our own times in many of the sacred Shrines throughout the Christian world.

[32] John 5:4.

PART II

OUR GUARDIAN ANGELS AND ANGELOPHANIES

Chapter VII

THE GUARDIAN ANGELS

A S God's messengers to men, the angelic ministry has been
often recorded in the sacred books of both the Old and the
New Testament. No less impressive is the record of their earthly
service in behalf of men that is found in the pages of Christian
hagiography. This second part shall study this aspect of the
angelic life and examine the various questions concerning our
Guardian Angels, angelophanies or manifestations of the Guardian Angel to some Saints, and some private and public devotions
to the Guardian Angels.

The Angels were appointed as guides and protectors, (the
Greek Fathers occasionally called them *pedagogues*), to men by
that Divine Providence Which watches over mankind from the
beginning: "He hath given his angels charge over thee, to keep
thee in all thy ways. In their hands they shall bear thee up, lest
thou dash thy foot against a stone. Thou shalt walk upon the
asp and the basilisk, and thou shalt trample under foot the
lion and the dragon."[1] These sacred words of the Psalmist
expressing angelic protection are referred primarily to Christ and
secondarily to all the faithful.

The words of the Lord promising the protection of an Angel
to His chosen people, on the long and difficult journey to the
Promised Land, are applied, in the liturgy of the Church, to the
Guardian Angels of individual souls: "Behold I will send my

[1] Ps. 90:11-13.

angel, who shall go before thee, and keep thee in thy journey, and bring thee into the place that I have prepared."[2] The Savior of mankind told His disciples that He was going to prepare a place for them in His Father's house,[3] in heaven, the land of the living, our promised land. The holy Angels whom a merciful Father has assigned to each of us shall escort us on this journey; they go before us protecting and defending and leading us in this life which, in many respects, resembles the long and weary journey of the Israelites through the desert.

Our Guardian Angels are the collaborators of Divine Providence in this world. Saint Paul calls them ministering spirits of our salvation: "Are they not all ministering spirits sent to minister for them, who shall receive the inheritance of salvation?"[4]

The Old Testament is not very explicit on the question of a personal Guardian Angel, as we understand it today; however, there was, even then, a firm belief that at least the saints and the just were under the protection of an Angel or Angels; thus we read of the patriarch Jacob: "Jacob also went on the journey he had begun, and the angels of God met him."[5] Traveling in those days was a difficult and dangerous adventure, hence the protection of the holy Angels is mentioned especially with traveling and with difficult missions. Similarly the special mission of the great national heroine, Judith: "His angel has been my keeper both going hence and abiding there and returning from thence hither."[6] These and similar individual cases reported in Sacred Scripture should not be regarded as exceptions, because the Psalmist says that the angelic protection belongs to the ordinary

---

[2] Exod. 23:20.

[3] John 14:2.

[4] Hebr. 1:14.

[5] Gen. 32:1. The apocryphal book of Henoch says that the just and the saints "have protecting spirits." (100, 5).

[6] Judith 13:20.

rule of Divine Providence: "The angel of the Lord shall encamp round about them that fear him, and shall deliver them."[7]

When Christ's disciples spoke of the Guardian Angel of Simon Peter, in a spontaneous and matter-of-fact remark, they were voicing a traditional belief which had been confirmed by the word of the Divine Savior Himself. The charming incident throws much light on the angelic power and manner of his operation, as well as on the life of the infant Church: "Peter was kept in prison, but prayer was made without ceasing by the church unto God for him."[8] The night preceding the day on which King Herod was to bring him forth for condemnation and execution, Peter was sleeping between two soldiers, bound with two chains, while the keepers stood watching before the door of the prison. The Lord wanted Peter free. He sent an Angel, or commanded Peter's own Angel to carry out the will of the Lord in this respect. The Angel put the two soldiers and the keepers of the prison to sleep; he made the two chains to fall from Peter's hands, then he ordered Peter to dress in a hurry and to follow him. Peter, of course, could not believe what he saw and thought that it was all a dream, but the Angel kept urging him to come out. As the Angel approached the prison doors they all swung open before him, including the iron door leading into the city, Jerusalem. Seeing himself free once again in the dark and narrow street which was completely deserted at that late hour of the night, and noticing that the Angel had disappeared from his sight, Simon Peter began to realize what had happened: "And Peter coming to himself said: Now I know for certain that the Lord has sent his angel and rescued me from the power of Herod and from all the expectation of the people of the Jews."[9] After a brief reflection on the situation, Simon Peter went

---

[7] Ps. 33:8.
[8] Acts 12:5.
[9] *Ibid.* 11.

to the house of Mary, who was the mother of his future companion, the Evangelist John Mark, where many faithful had gathered together in prayer. "When he knocked at the outer door, a maid named Rhoda came to answer it. And as soon as she recognized Peter's voice, in her joy she did not open the gate, but ran in and announced that Peter was standing before the gate. But they said to her, 'Thou art mad.' But she insisted that it was so. Then they said, 'It is his angel.' But Peter continued knocking; and when they opened, they saw him and were amazed."[10] It was humanly impossible for Peter to escape from prison; therefore, they thought, he could not be there in person. His Guardian Angel must have assumed his voice and his appearance.

The whole force of the argument taken from the remark of those earliest Jewish Christians is based not so much on the word "Angel" as on the pronoun "his": his Angel, his personal guardian and protector, his Guardian Angel, like the Angel of any other person in that prayerful gathering.

This then was the belief of the apostolic age concerning the Guardian Angels, in the beautiful words of Jesus concerning children: "See that you despise not one of these little ones, for I say to you that their Angels in heaven always see the face of my Father who is in heaven."[11] In saying, *their Angels,* the Divine Savior reveals the consoling truth that each child has a Guardian Angel, a blessed spirit from the court of heaven, to escort him through life. This truth must be believed with divine faith. From this truth theologians, with a simple but sound reasoning, come to the conclusion that not only children but also adult persons and old people have their Guardian Angel. The reasoning is more or less of this nature, and it may be called an argument *a fortiori:* Guardian Angels are given to little children, who usually enjoy all the care and protection of their parents, at an

---

[10] *Ibid.* 13-16.　　　[11] Matt. 18:10.

age when they cannot take care of themselves physically and when no spiritual dangers as yet threaten their immortal soul; when they grow up and are able to take care of themselves physically, greater physical and moral dangers threaten body and soul, at at time when they are left to themselves and are without parental protection. The Divine Providence that protected their tender bodies in childhood will certainly not abandon them to the fury of the enemies now that their immortal soul, with their body, is exposed to far greater dangers, especially when, as is often the case, the adult person has great responsibilities, as father or mother or as a supporter of wife and children and old parents. This, however, is more than a mere theological conclusion. Even though no formal dogmatic definition to this effect was ever made, it nevertheless remains a matter of faith that all men have a Guardian Angel, because this doctrine is taught by the common and ordinary teaching authority of the Universal Church and it reflects the doctrine of Scripture and of Christian Tradition.

This truth is thus expressed by F. Suarez, S.J., a great authority on this subject: "Even though Scripture does not affirm explicity the existence of Guardian Angels, nor has the Church defined this truth, it is nevertheless universally admitted, and it is so firmly based upon Scripture as interpreted by the Fathers, that its denial would be a very great rashness and practically an error."[12]

Commenting on these words of Christ, concerning the Angels of the little children, Saint Basil the Great says: "That each one of the faithful has an Angel who directs his life as a pedagogue and a shepherd, nobody can deny, remembering the words of our Lord: 'See that you despise not one of these little ones.' "[13]

---

[12] *De Angelis*, VI, 17: "ut sine ingenti temeritate et fere errore negari non possit."

[13] *Contra Eunomium*, III, 1.

Similar is the firm belief of Saint John Chrysostom, who refers to the faith of the old Patriarch Jacob: "Every faithful Christian," he writes, "has an Angel, for every just man had an Angel from the very beginning, as Jacob says: 'The Angel that nourisheth me and delivereth me from youth.' "[14] From these expressions of the Fathers, "every faithful," it is evident that they admitted the presence of a Guardian Angel not only for the little children but for the faithful of every age. In addition, that same expression should not be understood in the exclusive sense, excluding, namely, infidels and sinners. According to the majority of theologians, the Fathers generally regarded the Guardian Angels as instruments of Divine Providence in this world, and consequently their ministry extended to all souls redeemed by Christ: "Their (the Fathers') utterances must not be interpreted in an exclusive sense: these Fathers merely wish to emphasize that every good Christian enjoys the special protection of a Guardian Angel, which does not exclude that God bestows the same paternal providence also upon the heathen and the sinner."[15]

The consent of the Fathers concerning the privilege of a Guardian Angel for all, is lacking when we come down to more specific questions on the subject, such as the exact time in the life of the individual when the Guardian Angel assumes his duty; whether, not only Christians in the state of grace, but also sinners and pagans and other unbaptized persons share the same privilege. Concerning these questions we find often hesitation and difference of opinion with some ancient Christian writers, like Origen, and some of the Fathers. Origen, in his commentary on Matthew,[16] affirms that all men, both the faithful and the

---

[14] *Homil. in Col.,* 3:4.

[15] Pohle-Preuss, *God the Author of Nature and the Supernatural,* p. 336.

[16] *Commentary on Matthew,* XIII, 26.

unbelievers, have their Guardian Angel, whereas in his work
De Principiis he writes that only the faithful and those in the
state of grace have this privilege: "Each faithful, although the
humblest in the Church, is said to be attended by an angel who is
declared by the Savior always to behold the face of God the
Father, and as this angel was certainly one with the object of his
guardianship so, if the latter is rendered unworthy by want of
obedience, the Angel of God is said to be taken from him."[17]
Not only does Origen exclude sinners from the privilege of
angelic ministry, as in this text, but at one time he even denied it
to all the adults, as in the commentary on Saint Matthew, mentioned above, where he says that the Angels of the little ones remain with them as long as they are in need of "nursing fathers
and nursing mothers and guardians and stewards, but when they
have become perfect they are governed by the Lord."[18]

According to Saint Jerome the Guardian Angel is given at

[17] *De Principiis,* II, 10, 7.
[18] *Commentary on Matthew,* XIII, 28. Since we have been presenting
Origen's hesitation on this question we should not omit mentioning, in
this connection, his other extravagant and unorthodox opinion concerning
the conversion of a bad guardian angel or demon into a good Angel through
the conversion or baptism of the person in his charge: "It may be said
that there is no holy angel present with those who are still in wickedness,
but that during the period of unbelief they are under the angels of Satan;
but after regeneration, He who has redeemed us with His own blood
consigns us to a holy Angel, who also, because of his purity, beholds the
face of God. . . . As it is possible for a man to change from unbelief to
faith, and from intemperance to temperance, and generally from wickedness to virtue, so also it is possible that the angel, to whom any soul has
been entrusted at birth, may be wicked at first, but afterwards may at
some time believe in proportion as the man believes, and may make such
advance that he may become one of the angels who always behold the
face of the Father who is in heaven." This strange and erroneous opinion
is part of Origen's system, called *apocatastasis,* which was condemned in
the second Church Council of Constantinople in 553. It falsely assumes
that there is going to be a final restitution of all rational creatures, Satan
and all the demons and all lost souls regaining God's grace and His glory.
(*Denz.* 209, 211).

birth: "Great is the dignity of souls, so great indeed that each of them has an angel assigned for its protection from the moment it is born."[19] In this text Saint Jerome makes no distinction between the souls of the faithful and those of the infidels, between the souls of the just and those of the sinners. Every soul from the moment it is born in this world has a good angel, even before baptism and justification. Saint John Chrysostom shares the same opinion, in his commentary on the Acts of the Apostles.[20] Saint Basil[21] and Saint Cyril of Alexandria,[22] both limit the angelic ministry of a Guardian Angel to the faithful Christian souls. Saint Basil and Saint Jerome affirm that mortal sin puts the Angels into flight; and Saint Ambrose thinks that often the Lord deprives the just of the protection of his Guardian Angel in order to offer him an opportunity to fight alone and thus acquire more merit and consequently greater glory.[23]

This fluctuation of opinions with regard to secondary questions continued more or less throughout the patristic period. Greater harmony and unity of thought were reached by the Schoolmen on these and many other questions. Saint Thomas accepts the opinion of Saint Jerome with regard to the time when the Guardian Angel is given to the individual soul, and he states that the Angel is given at the time of birth and not at the time of baptism, because, he writes, the divine gifts which are given to man because he is a Christian begin at baptism, but the gifts which are given him because of his rational nature begin at birth, and such is the gift of a Guardian Angel.[24] Concerning the other

---

[19] *In Matt.* 18, 10.
[20] *Hom.* XXVI.
[21] *In Ps.* 35, 5.
[22] *De Adorat. in Spiritu,* IV.
[23] *In Ps.* 37, 43; 38, 32. St. Basil says that sin drives the Angels away like smoke does with bees and unpleasant odor with doves (*Hom. in Ps.* 33, 5).
[24] *Summa Theo.* I, Q. 113, art. 5.

question, whether the Angel leaves a man when he falls into sin, Saint Thomas is of the opinion that the Angel never abandons man completely, but sometimes the Angel may be said to leave man insofar as he does not prevent man from becoming involved in some tribulation, or even from falling into sin.[25]

The doctrine that holds that a Guardian Angel is given to all men is now the common opinion of Theologians. Even in his day, Suarez could affirm that the doctrine which says that not only the just but also the sinner, not only the faithful but also the unbeliever, not only the baptized but also the unbaptized have Guardian Angels reflects the common teaching of Theologians and the Fathers.[26]

From what we have said above regarding the teaching of the Fathers, a distinction should be made in this sense, that we find there an unanimous belief in the existence of Guardian Angels, but their opinions often differ widely with respect to secondary questions. However, enough ground is to be found there in support of the present common teaching of Theologians on these other questions. Saint Anselm, who in many respects was the forerunner of the great Schoolmen, had gone a step further when he declared that "every soul is committed to an Angel when it is united with the body."[27] Saint Thomas with other Schoolmen, following Saint Jerome and other Fathers, assigned the beginning of the mission of the Guardian Angel to time of birth rather than the time of animation, probably because during the time of gestation the Guardian Angel of the mother could very well take care also of the unborn child she was carrying, when the child was still, as it were, a part of herself, even though animated by a distinct soul, not unlike the unripe fruit which is part of the plant.

[25] *Ibid.* art. 6.
[26] *De Angelis,* VI, 17.
[27] *Elucid.,* II, 31.

As explained in the first part of this book, the name Angel is sometimes taken in a generic sense and it applies to all the various orders and ranks of the three heavenly Hierarchies, Seraphim, Cherubim, Thrones, etc: sometimes the name Angel is taken in a specific sense and it applies to the lowest Choir or rank, the third Angelic Hierarchy which consists of Principalities, Archangels, and Angels. This distinction is very important for the solution of our next question. The question is this: From what Choir of what Hierarchy do our Guardian Angels come? According to Dionysius, the first and greatest authority on the subject, they are taken from the third and lowest Angelic Hierarchy, namely from the Principalities, the Archangels, and the Angels: "The highest Hierarchy, being in the foremost place near the Hidden One [God], must be regarded as hierarchically ordering in a mysterious manner the second Hierarchy; and the Hierarchy of Dominations, Virtues, and Powers leads the Principalities, Archangels, and Angels more manifestly indeed than the first Hierarchy, . . . and the revealing Hierarchy of the Principalities, Archangels, and Angels presides one through the other over the human hierarchies so that their elevation and turning to God and their communion and union with Him may be in order . . . accordingly the Word of God has our [namely the earthly or Ecclesiastical] hierarchy in the care of Angels, for Michael is called Prince of the people of Juda, and other Angels are assigned to other peoples."[28] The great majority of the Schoolmen follow the opinion of Dionysius and hold that the Guardian Angels are taken from the third Hierarchy consisting of Principalities, Archangels and Angels, these heavenly spirits being the closest to the earthly and human order of Divine Providence. The name Angel, which means messenger, applies to these three lower Choirs in a very special manner, because they are the ones whom God has sent from time to time into

[28] *The Celest. Hier.,* IX.

this world; these are His legates with man, His Angels. Seraphim, Cherubim, and the higher heavenly Choirs are closest to the throne of God and have duties entirely different from our earthly and human conditions and interests. Suarez follows the same opinion in his celebrated work on the Angels.[29] Duns Scotus and his School generally admit that the Guardian Angels and all the Angels sent by God to deal with human beings in this world, may be taken, and are taken, from any and all the Choirs of Angels, including the very highest. This opinion which is very dear to a number of saints and mystical souls is said to be based upon the words of Saint Paul in his Epistle to the Hebrews, where speaking of Angels he remarks: "Are they not all ministering spirits, sent to minister for them, who shall receive the inheritance of salvation."[30] According to the defenders of this opinion the word "Angel," in this text, is to be understood in a generic sense as applying to all the Choirs and the entire angelic world. However, from the purpose and intention of the inspired writer, as is evident from the context, the word "Angel," in this case, has to be taken in a very specific sense, particularly for those Angels who promulgated the Old Law on Mount Sinai: "You who have received the law dictated by Angels and did not keep it."[31] At the time this Epistle was dictated by Saint Paul, the Jewish Christians were on the verge of apostasy and of falling back to Moses, their contention being that the Mosaic Law was superior to the new law, the law of Christ, because it had been given to Moses by Angels. Saint Paul, in the first two chapters of this Epistle, contrasts the Son of God, as author of the new Covenant, with those Angels who revealed the old Covenant on Mount Sinai, and shows Christ's superiority to Moses and to the Angels who revealed the Old Law

[29] *De Angelis,* VI, 10.
[30] Hebr. 1:14.
[31] Acts 7:53.

to him. In the second verse of the second chapter of this same Epistle, Saint Paul writes: "For if the word, spoken by angels, proved to be valid and every transgression and disobedience received a just punishment, how shall we escape if we neglect so great a salvation?" The transcending superiority of Christ to these Angels implies superiority of the law of Christ over the Law of Moses, of the New Testament over the Old. From all this we gather that the Angels mentioned here in these two chapters, and specifically in the text brought forward in support of their opinion,[32] are the Angels who were instrumental in revealing the Law of Moses. Nobody would suppose that this revelation of the Old Law was made by those myriads and myriads of heavenly spirits that form the Angelic world. We have seen in the first part how one single Angel was able to kill a whole army of one hundred and eighty five thousand soldiers, in one night. There seems, therefore, to be no reason to assign millions upon millions of Angels to a much simpler task, that of dictating the Law of Moses.

Regardless of the pious meditations and ideas of some Saints, like Saint Mathilde, Saint Gertrude, Saint Hildegarde, and the opinions of Tauler, Denys the Carthusian and a few others, we believe that the Guardian Angels are ordinarily taken from the Choir of Angels, sometimes from that of the Archangels, and only exceptionally, if ever, from the Choir of Principalities, all belonging to the lowest of the three Angelic Hierarchies. This opinion is more in accordance with Scripture and Tradition and it still remains the more common opinion of Theologians. "The Angels fill up and complete the lowest Choir of all the Hierarchies of the celestial intelligences since they are the last of the celestial beings possessing the angelic nature. And they indeed are more properly named Angels by us than are those of a higher rank because their choir is more directly in contact with

[32] Hebr. 1:14.

manifested and earthly things."[33] Saint Thomas closely follows
the doctrine of Dionysius, as Saint Gregory the Great had
done before him, and concludes his article on this subject with
the words: "We must simply say with Dionysius that the higher
Angels are never sent out for external [i.e., earthly] ministry."[34]
To this we may add that if the higher Angels are never sent out
on an earthly mission, much less would they be employed for
a lifelong service as Guardian Angels. Their mission is not one
of messengers and legates but as attendants at the court of
heaven, and the nature of this, their mission, remains as much
a mystery to us as the life of heaven itself.

[33] Dionysius, *op. cit.*
[34] *Op. cit.*, Q. 112, art. 2.

Chapter VIII

THE GUARDIAN ANGELS
OF NATIONS AND OF CHURCHES

ACCORDING to Saint Thomas, neither man nor any other thing can remain entirely outside the government of Divine Providence.[1] This fundamental principle was applied, by some of the early Christian writers and Fathers, in a rather exaggerated manner, so as to require a particular Angel for everything in this world: all the elements, the stars of heaven, every living thing, including insects.[2] Origen denies, indeed, the influence of demons on everything we Christians use, but he admits a corresponding influence and protection of invisible guardians, whom he later calls divine Angels: "We indeed do also maintain with regard not only to the fruits of the earth, but to every flowing stream and every breath of air, that the ground brings forth those things which are said to grow up naturally, that the water springs in fountains and refreshes the earth with running streams, that the air is kept pure, and supports the life of those who breathe it, only in consequence of the agency and control of certain beings whom we may call invisible husbandmen and guardians, but we deny that those invisible agents are demons."[3] Saint Thomas and the Schoolmen reject this opinion as exaggerated, but they ordinarily admit as probable that one

[1] *Summa Theo.*, I, Q. 113, art. 6.
[2] Origen, *In Jer. Hom.* X, 6; St. Ambrose, *In Ps. 118, Serm.* I, 9 and 12; St. Augustine, *De Lib. Arb.*, III, 32.
[3] *Contra Celsum*, VIII, 31.

Angel is in charge of each entire species of living things, outside of man, because according to the same Providence it is the species that is destined to survive and continue indefinitely; for which, they thought, a special protection was needed. "All the Angels who are in charge of purely corporeal things seem to belong to the choir of Virtues; even miracles sometimes happen through the ministry of these same angels."[4]

Since the Angels are ministers of Divine Providence in this world, it would seem that not only the life and existence of individual human beings should be placed under their protection but also that of nations, cities, Churches and communities.

The Septuagint version of Deuteronomy, chapter 32:8, which reads: "When the Most High divided the nations, as He separated the sons of Adam, He set the bounds of nations according to the angels of God," (the Vulgate has: "he set the bounds of people according to the number of the children of Israel"), must have offered the Greek Christian writers with a firm basis for the belief that nations and cities, in addition to individuals are under the protection of guardian Angels. Thus, among others, Clement of Alexandria: "Regiments of Angels are distributed over nations and cities, and, perchance, some are assigned to individuals."[5] However, it is in the vision of the Prophet Daniel that we find a more solid basis for this truth. In this vision the Prophet reveals that three nations, the Israelites, the Persians, and the Greeks had each a national tutelary or guardian Angel whom he calls prince.[6] This name probably implies that the national Guardian Angel belongs to the highest Choir of the lowest Hierarchy (Principalities, Archangels, Angels), the Choir of Principalities, or more probably that they are Archangels; yet in the quality of Guardian of nations they

[4] *Op. cit.*, Q. 110, art. 1.
[5] *Stromata*, VI, 17.
[6] Dan. 10:13 ff.

are called Princes. This is certainly the case with the Archangel Michael whom Daniel calls Prince of the Jewish nation: "Dost thou know wherefore I am come to thee?" asks the Archangel who has just appeared to the Prophet Daniel, "and now I will return to fight against the prince of the Persians. When I went forth there appeared the prince of the Greeks coming. But I will tell thee what is set down in the scripture of truth: and none is my helper in all these things, but Michael your prince."[7] This Angel who has been talking to Daniel was actually the Archangel Gabriel. He says that he is going to fight against the prince of the Persians, that means, he is going to fight against the national Guardian Angel of the Persians. In going forth he saw the national Guardian Angel of the Greeks coming, but it seems that he did not succeed in obtaining help from him. The only one who had helped and assisted him in his holy battle was Saint Michael the Archangel, the Guardian Angel of the Jewish nation of those days. This charming revelation made by one of the great heavenly spirits, the Archangel Gabriel, may disconcert us a little. After all how can we reconcile the unchangeable charity and harmony and peace existing among heavenly spirits with fighting and wars, which usually imply enmity and discord. Yet, there is no doubt that this talk of war and fighting refers to love and zeal for the salvation of the people committed to their care. Each national protecting Angel sought the spiritual advantage and the salvation of the people of his territory, as duty demanded. The Archangel Gabriel (to whom Daniel had prayed for the liberation of the Jewish people from the captivity in which they were still being kept by the Persians) had secured the assistance of the Archangel Michael, national Guardian Angel of the Jewish nation, in promoting the liberation of the Jews from captivity, but he had found a powerful opponent to his efforts in the national Guar-

[7] *Ibid.* 20.

dian Angel, or prince, of the Persians, who resisted all the attempts of Gabriel and Michael with the purpose of keeping the Jews in captivity much longer. This great Angel of the Persian people, who were a pagan nation that did not believe in the true God, had noticed the many blessings that the presence of those faithful captive Jews had brought to the Persians, whereby many of these had found the way of salvation. He, therefore, wanted that those blessings should continue for the good of his wards, and resisted with all his love and might the efforts of the other Angels, who were concerned with the interests of their nations. It was a battle of love perfectly compatible with peace and charity. Each Angel knows what God wants him to do for the people of his territory, but without special revelation he does not know exactly what God expects from the Angel of another nation, hence their differences. Yet, all their missions are carried out with great firmness and mutual love— for the glory of God and the peace of men. The Prophet Daniel uses here a language of wars and contentions to express the ardent zeal and interest which are displayed by these Angels in the fulfillment of their duty as national protective spirits.[8]

If pagan nations of old, such as Persia and Greece, were under the protection of an Angel, how much more should we expect such protection upon Christian nations. Hence Saint John Damascene, summing up the opinion of the Fathers, his predecessors, writes: "They [the Angels] also guard parts of this earth; they preside over nations and regions, according as they have been appointed by the supreme creator."[9] If civil and political units, such as cities and nations enjoy the privilege of a Guardian Angel, ecclesiastical units, like dioceses, parishes, churches, demand a similar protection, for the simple reason that these

---

[8] St. Thomas treats of this subject in *Summa Theo.* I, Q. 113, art. 8, under the title: Utrum inter Angelos possit esse pugna seu discordia.

[9] *De Fide Orthod.* II, 3.

are integral parts and units of the Kingdom of God here on earth. In writing to the seven Churches of Asia Minor, at the beginning of his Apocalypse, Saint John the Evangelist is commanded to address his messages to the seven Angels of the seven churches: "The seven stars are the angels of the seven churches. And the seven candlesticks are the seven churches."[10] It is true that common interpretation holds that it is to the local bishop that the message is to be addressed, as the Angel of each of the seven churches. Although the bishop is meant, it is really to the local Guardian Angel, the witness of the bishop's conduct and protector of that church, to whom the message is addressed. In fact, if the "seven stars are the angels of the seven churches" how could we call a star the bishop of the church of Sardis of whom it is said: "I know thy works, that thou hast the name of being alive, and thou art dead";[11] or what shining star was the bishop of the church of Laodicea, whom the Lord was about "to vomit out," because he was wretched, and miserable, and poor, and blind, and naked. The seven stars were, therefore, the seven Guardian Angels of those seven churches, through whom and in whose name notice was served to the respective bishop of what the Lord thought of him and expected of him. We believe, therefore, that these texts of the first three chapters of the Apocalypse, are a classical example of this truth, and a solid argument in favor of the doctrine we are presenting. The Angel of the church is a real Angel, the heavenly guardian and protector of that community whom the human minister, bishop or priest, should imitate, and to whom he should pray with his flock.

Another reference to this category of Guardian Angels can be found in the prophecy of the Prophet Zacharias where he writes: "And I said: What are these my Lord? and the angel

---

[10] Apoc. 1:20.   [11] *Ibid.* 3:1.

that spoke in me, said to me: I will show thee what these are. And the man [an angel in the shape of man] that stood among the myrtle trees answered and said: These are they whom the Lord hath sent to walk through the earth. And they answered the angel of the Lord that stood among the myrtle trees, and said: We have walked through the earth and behold all the earth is inhabited, and at rest. And the angel of the Lord answered and said: O Lord of hosts, how long wilt thou not have mercy on Jerusalem, and on the cities of Juda, with which thou hast been angry? this is now the seventieth year."[12] The man standing among the myrtle trees, and who is later called Angel, was the national Guardian Angel of the Jews, the Archangel Michael. He is the one who is praying to the Lord of hosts to be merciful to Jerusalem and the cities of Juda which had been in a state of desolation for seventy years. How well did this prince of the heavenly hosts fulfill his mission of national protector and intercessor for the people committed to his care! To the same category belong those other Angels mentioned in this prophecy: "Those whom the Lord hath sent to walk through the earth." These, too, were guardians of territories, nations, and peoples, hence their interest in the fact that the earth was inhabited and was at rest.

The vision that Saint Paul had of a mysterious man from Macedonia "standing and beseeching him" to pass over into Macedonia and help them,[13] is commonly interpreted as being the vision of the Guardian Angel of the country and the people of Macedonia. The promptness with which Paul obeyed that call shows that he must have been convinced that the Macedonian who had appeared to him was actually a messenger of God, an Angel: "And as soon as he had seen the vision, immediately

12 Zach. 1:9-12.
13 Acts 16:9.

we sought to go into Macedonia, being assured that God had called us to preach the gospel to them."[14]

Saint Thomas, with a number of other theologians, is of the opinion that public persons, like rulers of nations, governors of states or of large communities both civil and ecclesiastic, such as Ordinary Bishops, Abbots, etc., besides their own Guardian Angel, received at birth, are given another, an additional Angel, when they assume the responsibilities of such an office, who will then assist them in the government and administration of the people committed to their care.[15]

Just as the Synagogue of old, so is the Church of God (our Mother Church which is the Kingdom of God on earth) under the protection of the Holy Angels; and Saint Michael the Archangel is the heavenly protector of the Christian people as he had been of the Jewish people in the Old Testament. "O Mother Church" writes Saint Bernard, "your guardians are the holy Angels!"[16] He also believed that every Christian edifice, every church or chapel where divine services are held is under the care of holy Angels.[17] Saint Paul seems to refer to the presence of the Angels in Christian assemblies for prayer, in our churches, when he requires that all Christian women cover their head in such places "because of the angels."[18]

[14] *Ibid.* 10.
[15] *II Sent.,* D. 14, q. 1, art. 2 ad 4 et 5.
[16] *In Cant. Cant., Sermo* 77, 4.
[17] *In Dedic. Eccl., Sermo* 4, 2 f.
[18] I Cor. 11:10.

Chapter IX

WHAT GUARDIAN ANGELS DO FOR US

IN the Catholic doctrine on Guardian Angels we find one of the most touching traits of Divine Love and Divine Providence in behalf of man. Saint Bernard of Clairvaux grew most eloquent whenever writing or speaking about our Guardian Angels: "O wonderful condescension of God! O love truly marvelous! . . . The Most High has commanded the Angels, his Angels, those sublime spirits, so blessedly happy and so near his throne, his familiar, his closest friends. He has given his Angels charge over thee. Who art thou? *What is man, that thou art mindful of him? . . .* And what thinkest thou he has ordered them in thy account?—To protect thee."[1]

Nothing reminds man more vividly of his superior spiritual nature and of his glorious destiny in heaven than this unseen heavenly escort given us during our earthly pilgrimage. Just as kings give their children a tutor, an attendant from their own court, so the King of Heaven has given men, His adoptive children through grace, tutelary spirits, guardians and protectors from His own court.

What are, in particular, the duties of our Guardian Angels? Analyzing these duties, Saint Bernard says that the Angels constantly surround the souls of the faithful in their charge with the most tender care and love. They have but one great desire, that of leading us safely through life till we attain the glory and

[1] *In Ps. Qui inhabitat,* Sermo XII, 3-5.

peace which they themselves possess and fully enjoy while in our company here on earth. They protect both our spiritual and our corporal life. They defend and protect our immortal soul from the seduction of the world and the wiles of Satan. They often shield us from sudden dangers that threaten our life, or come to our rescue when some harm has befallen us. This becomes often manifest with little children who quite often come out of serious accidents without any injury. The mind of the little children cannot be reached with warnings and inspirations, because it is not yet functioning; and thus the Guardian Angel must take direct action in case of danger. Adult persons, in the full use of reason, are warned and cautioned by their Angel, but because they remain free to heed or to ignore such warnings of their Angel, many unfortunate things happen to them in spite of their heavenly protector.

The most important of all the duties of a Guardian Angel is that of positively helping man in the tremendous work of saving his immortal soul. They accomplish this by exciting in our hearts pious and salutary thoughts and desires or, at times, salutary fear of God's judgments. They become intermediaries between God and man, as they lay our needs and our fears before Him, offering God our desires and our prayers, and in return they bring us His grace and His gifts.[2] The often-mentioned activity of the Archangel Raphael, in favor of old Tobias and his son, is the best illustration of the manifold duties of a Guardian Angel. The entire book *Tobias* gives us not only an example of patience and charity in the holy man Tobias, but also reveals to us the wonderful and loving ministry of our Guardian Angels.

Occasionally the Angel, in order to give us an opportunity to do penance and to atone for our faults, allows that trials and suffering come our way, or that violent temptations humble our pride and warn us in our complacency. Thus they are truly

[2] St. Bernard, *In Cant.*, Sermo XXII, 5; XXXI, 5.

Pedagogues, as the Greek Fathers often called them, or, better still, spiritual masters and directors. We read often in the life of some Saints who enjoyed the privilege of seeing with their bodily eyes their Guardian Angel almost constantly (as was the case with Saint Frances of Rome and Saint Gemma Galgani, as we shall report later in this book), that the Angel often disappeared from their sight, either to try them or to punish them for some little fault they had committed; the devil would then appear and afflict them in various manners.

Indirectly, the Angels help man by keeping the devil away or at least restraining him from causing all the harm and the spiritual ruin which he so persistently tries to bring upon us, not excluding physical violence and even death. Thus they eliminate many occasions of sin, reduce the number of temptations, and break their force, and in this manner they actually fulfill in our behalf what, in a symbolical language, was expressed in Psalm 90: "In their hands they [the Angels] shall bear thee up; lest thou dash thy foot against a stone. Thou shalt walk upon the asp and the basilisk; and thou shalt trample under foot the lion and the dragon."[3] The lion, in this text, is actually the devil himself, of whom Saint Peter writes: "Your adversary the devil, as a roaring lion, goeth about seeking whom he may devour."[4] The dragon again is another name for Satan: "That great dragon was cast out, that old serpent, who is called the devil and Satan, who seduceth the world, and he was cast out unto the earth."[5] Against all these invisible enemies of mankind stands as shield and protection our Guardian Angel whose struggles and victories are known to God alone.

Our Guardian Angels pray for us and with us, and they offer our prayers, our suffering, and our good desires to the throne of

---

[3] Ps. 90:12 f.
[4] I Pet. 5:8.
[5] Apoc. 12:9.

God. This most consoling truth is revealed by the glorious
Archangel Raphael: "I discover then the truth unto you, and
I will not hide the secret from you. When thou didst pray with
tears, and didst bury the dead, and didst leave thy dinner and hide
the dead by day in thy house, and bury them at night, I offered
thy prayer to the Lord."[6] We see here how this Archangel offered
not only Tobias' prayers but also his tears, his great works of
mercy, his self-denial in leaving his dinner untouched in order to
bury the dead. For all this, Tobias had received nothing but
great trials and finally blindness: "And because thou wast acceptable to God, it was necessary that temptation should prove
thee."[7] No doubt the Archangel who watched over Tobias so
carefully could have prevented the accident that caused his blindness, but he did not, in order to offer him an occasion for even
greater virtue and more merit.

Another duty of our Angels is that of praising God, and they
wish us to join them in this heavenly occupation. This is the
first thing that the Archangel Raphael demanded before revealing his identity: "Bless ye the God of heaven, give glory to
him in the sight of all that live, because he has shown his mercy
to you."[8] When the faithful soul, leaving this mortal body, shall
look for the first time upon the enchanting features of her heavenly guide and try to offer thanks for his loving service, she will
probably hear the same answer that the grateful Tobias received
from the Archangel Raphael: "Peace be to you, fear not; for
when I was with you, I was there by the will of God: bless
ye him, and sing praises to him!"[9]

The loving kindness of our Guardian Angels is such that they
often go on errands here on earth in behalf of their proteges, or

[6] Tob. 12:11 f.
[7] *Ibid.* 13.
[8] *Ibid.* 6.
[9] *Ibid.* 17 f.

help them with their work. This feature of their ministry will be explained with actual examples in the following chapter. Suffice it here to mention a well-known custom, in our day, with devout persons who have met the saintly Padre Pio of Pietrelcina, the stigmatic Capuchin priest living at S. Giovanni Rotondo, Italy: When in need of spiritual assistance or in order to ask for prayer, they—at Padre Pio's suggestion—send their own Guardian Angel to him and often with happy results. It is reported by one, associated with the good Padre, that one morning he complained about the constant arrival of Guardian Angels with various petitions during the night, saying: "Those Guardian Angels didn't let me sleep a moment last night!"

It is at the hour of death that the good Angel shows the greatest zeal in protecting and defending the soul committed to his care, invoking often the assistance of other Angels against the wiles and the fury of Satan. According to Origen, "At the hour of death the celestial escort (psychopompe) receives the soul the moment it leaves the body."[10] This common Christian belief, of the soul being accompanied by its Angel to the Divine Tribunal is based on the words of Our Lord: "And it came to pass, that the beggar died, and was carried by the angels into Abraham's bosom."[11] The same truth finds expression in the liturgical prayers of the Church, especially in the burial service for adults: "May the Angels lead thee into Paradise, may the Martyrs receive thee at thy coming, and take thee to Jerusalem the holy City. May the choirs of the Angels receive thee, and mayest thou with the once poor Lazarus have rest everlasting. . . . Come to his assistance ye Saints of God; meet him ye Angels of the Lord. Receive his soul and present it to the Most High. May Christ who called thee receive thee, and may the Angels lead thee into the bosom of Abraham."

[10] *In Johan.*, XIX, 4.
[11] Luke 16:22.

Should the departed soul be not quite ready to enter heaven because it has not fully satisfied Divine Justice for its faults, and must therefore remain for some time in Purgatory, the Guardian Angel will lead it to the place of expiation. The same Angel will often visit it and comfort it in company of other good Angels.[12] In the meantime, while the soul is suffering in Purgatory, the Guardian Angel goes around inspiring and prompting some of the friends and relatives or other good souls here on earth to pray and to offer Masses for its release from Purgatory. The Guardian Angel will not rest till the day when he shall introduce the soul into Paradise, where it can share with him the blessed vision of God and join in the never-ending hymn of praise and thanksgiving to the Lord of Heaven.

[12] Suarez, *De Angelis,* VI, 19.

Chapter X

ANGELOPHANIES OR ANGELIC MANIFESTATIONS

BY Angelophany we understand a sensible manifestation or visible apparition of Angels. A good many of these Angelophanies have been reported in the preceding chapters of this book, all of them taken from the sacred books of the Bible. In all those cases we had the divine authority of the inspired word of God vouching for the truth of the alleged apparitions of Angels.

Similar reports of Angelic manifestations are found in Christian hagiography. In the life story of many of our Saints we often read of Angels appearing to them and conversing with them, ordinarily the Angel being the Guardian Angel of that Saint. Obviously, all these Angelophanies differ from those reported in Sacred Scripture, because they rest entirely and solely on human authority and, therefore, cannot compare with any of those reported in the Sacred Books. The historical evidence is not always the same in these reports of private visions and apparitions of Angels. Those, for example, that are found in the unauthentic acts of the Martyrs are often fictitious or legendary. Yet, we do possess some very well documented accounts of Angelophanies which we regard as authentic and very reliable cases of this sort.

If Angelic apparitions are found all through the Old Testament, during the life of Christ and his apostles, should we be surprised if we saw them continued all through the centuries of history of Christianity, which, after all, is the history of the Kingdom of God on earth?

The church historian Theodoret confirms the reports of the Angelic apparitions made to Saint Simeon Stylites, who lived for thirty-seven years on the narrow summit of a sixty foot high pillar, where he was often and visibly visited by his Guardian Angel, who instructed him about the mysteries of God and of the eternal life and spent many hours, at a time, with him in holy conversations and finally foretold him the day on which he would die.[1]

In their apparitions, the Angels do not only comfort the weary soul by the kindness and wisdom of their words, the beauty and loveliness of their features, but they often delight and lift up the fallen spirit by the sweetest music and heavenly melodies. We read often of such manifestations in the life of saintly monks of old. Mindful of the words of the Psalmist: "In the sight of Angels I will sing praise unto Thee,"[2] and of the advice of their holy founder Saint Benedict,[3] some holy monks actually found themselves chanting the holy office, at night, in the midst of Angels, who joined their heavenly voices to the human singing. The Venerable Bede, who often quoted the above passage of the Rule of Saint Benedict, was firmly convinced of the presence of Angels in Monasteries: "I know," he said, one day, "that the Angels come to the canonical hours and visit our monastic communities; what would they say if they did not find me there among my brethren?"[4] In the Monastery of Saint-Riquier, both the Abbot Gervin and a number of his monks actually heard the Angels blend their heavenly voices to the chant of the monks, one night, with the sweetest strains, while the entire sanctuary was suddenly filled with the most delicate perfumes.[5] Saint John

[1] *Acta Sanctorum,* Jan. 1.
[2] Ps. 137:1.   [4] *L'Ascèce Benedictine,* p. 161.
[3] *The Holy Rule of St. Benedict,* XIX. [5] *Ibid.*

Gualbert, founder of the Vallombrosan monks, for three consecutive days before he died saw himself surrounded by Angels who assisted him and sang heavenly praises. Saint Nicholas of Tolentino, for six months before he died, was granted the joy of hearing every night the singing of Angels, thus increasing in him the ardent desire of going to heaven.

More than a dream, it was an imaginative vision, what Saint Francis of Assisi saw and heard the night he was unable to find any rest: "All will be as in heaven," he said to comfort himself, "there at least there is eternal peace and happiness," and in so saying he fell asleep. Then he noticed that an Angel stood by his bed holding a violin and bow in his hand. "Francis," said the heavenly spirit, "I will play for you as we play before the throne of God in heaven." Here the Angel placed the violin to his chin and drew the bow across the strings only a single time. Brother Francis was filled with so much joy and his soul experienced such a living sweetness, that it was as if he had a body no longer, and knew of no secret sorrow. "And if the Angel had drawn the bow down across the strings again," he told the Brothers next morning, "then would my soul have left my body from uncontrollable happiness."[6]

More often, however, the Guardian Angel assumes the role of a spiritual guide, a master of the spiritual life, or spiritual director, leading the soul to Christian perfection, and using all the means indicated to that effect, not excluding very severe corrections and punishments. We could mention scores of examples of this nature, but we must limit ourselves to mentioning a few very outstanding ones. Of such a nature was the visible ministry of the Guardian Angel of Saint Lidwina of Shiedham, Saint Rose of Lima, Saint Margaret of Cortona, Saint Frances of Rome, and especially Saint Gemma Galgani.

[6] *Fioretti,* II e III *Consider.*

Saint Margaret of Cortona (d. 1297)

In her youth Margaret had led a life of sin for about nine years, but startled by the violent death of him with whom she had sinned, she resolved to do penance for the rest of her life. She then gave herself, under the direction of Franciscan Fathers, to prayer, mortification, and to mercilessly chastising the flesh, persevering in these efforts till death. The Lord not only forgave the evil she had done but raised her to great sanctity and endowed her with mystical graces and the privilege of a sensible and very frequent apparition of her Guardian Angel, who instructed her and reassured her of God's love for her. When she could not understand how God could give such consolations, light, and charisms to a sinner, our Lord and His Angel came to reassure her: "I have been darkness; I have been darker than night!" cried Margaret, and Christ replied to her: "For love of you, new light, I bless the little cell where you live concealed in My love." The Guardian Angel helped Margaret become aware of the mystical road to be traveled, and he even marked for her the various stages of the ascent to the Father of light. The Angel said to her one day: "You are like a house which has been set on fire; it will burn until it is completely consumed; thus you will remain in the fire of tribulation to the very end. Surrounded as you are by peace, you actually live in a state of war. Remember that gold is purified in the furnace." After a while the Angel developed the basic idea of his instruction and brought it from the lower level of suffering to the loftier one of love of God and union with Him: "God waits for the heart and He makes it careful from the time of love's first desire. When that love demands Him ardently, He no longer defers returning to the soul. Love then achieves in a moment what is accomplished only with time in souls of less ardent charity." Here the Angel, as a good spiritual director speaks of the various degrees of the love of God, which are more or less the well-known degrees of purgation, illumination, and union: "There are three degrees," said the Angel, "in this pure love whereby the faithful and fervent soul draws her God to herself. When the soul considers herself destitute of all divine love, nothing can comfort her but God. It is then that the Most High inclines and sympathizes with the poor creature who has been given over to anguish . . . but before the common Father of all goes into the soul that He has created and redeemed, love purifies the heart of all its illusions. The third degree of love is a desire which inflames the spirit like fire. In this final state the soul never ceases to seek her beloved, her spouse, everywhere and in everything."[7]

Saint Frances of Rome (d. 1440)

Born of a noble family in Rome, in 1384, she, at the early age of twelve, was given in marriage to Lorenzo Ponziani and became the mother of several children. Favored by God with a high gift of long and frequent prayer, she nevertheless knew how to leave her devotions and to find God in her household work. By her example she did much in correcting the luxurious and idle mode of life of the Roman matrons. She stood faithfully by her husband in his many troubles and exiles; and after his death, in 1436, she joined, as a humble member, the community of the Institute of the Oblates which she herself had founded. She was favored with continual vision of her Angel. This is how it started.

In the year 1411, Saint Frances' first son, Evangelista, almost nine years old was near death. He had been a saintly and innocent child. Just before expiring, he smiled at his mother and said: "Behold the Angels who have come to take me to heaven! Mother, I will remember you!"

[7] *Acta Sanct.,* Feb. 3. *St. Margarite de Cortone,* by François Mauriac, **XXXIII.**

Exactly one year from the day that the young Evangelista had died, Saint Frances was spending the whole night in prayer in the Oratory of her palace in Rome. At the break of dawn, the Oratory was filled with a brilliant light, and in that light she saw her little son, Evangelista: the same lovely features, wearing the same clothes, but supremely beautiful and resplendent. At his side was another boy more beautiful and more glorious; yet Frances had eyes only for her dear son. With open arms the little Evangelista greeted his mother and said: "I am with the Angels of the second Choir of the first Hierarchy, together with this my young companion, who, as you see, is much more beautiful and resplendent than myself. He is an Archangel and in heaven he occupies a place above mine. God sends him to you, dear mother, to be of comfort to you in this life, on your earthly pilgrimage. He will not leave you night or day, and you shall have the sweet satisfaction of seeing him constantly with your bodily eyes." As the light of the new day was now filling the Oratory, the soul of young Evangelista said to his mother: "It is God's will that I return to heaven; the sight of this Archangel, who will remain with you, shall remind you of me." With a sweet smile he disappeared. The vision had lasted a whole hour.

Left alone, Frances turned her eyes and saw the blessed Archangel standing, his hands crossed on his chest. Trembling she fell on her knees, adoring and thanking the merciful God for such an extraordinary gift. She begged the blessed spirit, now made visible to her, to enlighten her in her doubts, to assist her in her difficulties, to defend her against the assaults of the devil, and to be her guide on the way of perfection, making her more and more acceptable in the eyes of God. Even though this Archangel did not reveal to her all the splendor of glory that is his in Paradise, the brilliant light of his countenance was such that Frances could not gaze on him without hurting her eyes; she, therefore, avoided fixing her eyes on the Angel himself and looked rather on the glow of light that surrounded him. Occasionally she was given power to contemplate his features directly, especially in time of prayer, when troubled by the devil, or when she spoke of the Angel to her own Confessor. On these special occasions the Angel seemed to dim somewhat the light that surrounded him, and this enabled Frances to look the Angel directly in the face. She saw that he resembled in stature a boy of nine, only a little taller than the ordinary child of that age. He had lively and sparkling eyes and the sweetest expression on his lovely face. He wore a white tunic and over it a tunicle, that reached to his feet, clear as light and of an ethereal color, something like sky-blue and flaming red. His hair was like spun gold, long enough to cover his neck and shoulders. The brilliant light that came from his hair was such that Frances was able to read her Office at night, or go through the house most safely as at midday, without the use of any candle or any other light. The Angel's power seemed to be in his hair; so that when the devil came around to trouble Saint Frances, the Angel shook his hair and this was sufficient to put the devil into flight and make him tremble. In the light shed by her Angel, Saint Frances saw the secret thoughts of men around her and the evil machinations of the devil. She noticed how this Angel sometimes walked or stood at her right side, sometimes on her left side, and sometimes over her head. Once this Angel stopped the hand of one member of the Institute of Oblates, founded by Saint Frances, who had tried to take her own life.

The day on which Frances joined her own community, in 1436, she had a vision in which she saw our Lord seated on a high throne and surrounded by myriads of Angels. When the Angelic Choir of the Powers came to the Lord, He appointed one of the highest spirits in their rank to be henceforth Frances' special guardian in place of the Archangel who had assisted her for the last twenty-four years. In his assumed human form this holy spirit was in every respect more beautiful and resplendent than the Archangel. He wore a dalmatic of a more precious appearance. He manifested far greater power and courage. His presence alone was enough to put into flight any evil spirit. In his left hand he carried three golden palm branches, the symbols of charity, firmness, and prudence, three virtues he thus constantly inculcated to Saint Frances.[8]

Neither the Archangel who assisted Saint Frances for twenty-four years, nor the Angelic Power that stayed with her for the last four years of her life, was her own Guardian Angel received at birth. These two were additional Angels, who according to Saint Thomas, are given to persons having the government or direction of people, and these are often taken from a higher Choir, as in this case.

Saint Gemma Galgani (1878-1903)

We can say without fear of exaggeration that the visible ministry of the Guardian Angel was never more admirable and better attested than in the life of Saint Gemma Galgani. She lived in our modern times, at the beginning of the present century. Her various gifts and especially the visible work of her Guardian Angel were put to a test more than once by her spiritual director, Fr. Germano di S. Stanislao, C.P., a very cultured priest, and a very prudent and enlightened guide. Whatever is found in fragmentary form in the life of other Saints, is met here in the fullest and most charming development imaginable. We shall quote extensively from the sources, which are primarily, Saint Gemma's *Diary, Autobiography,* her *Letters,* her transcribed ecstasies, her *Life* written by Fr. Germano di S.

---

[8] *Acta Sanct.,* Mar. 2. *Santa Francesca Romana,* by C. Albergotti, esp. chapters 6, 7, 32.

Stanislao, C.P., and the testimony of members of the family in which she lived as a guest, or adopted member, till she died. Most of our quotations from these works were translated directly from the original Italian.

Gemma saw her Angel constantly with her bodily eyes; they spoke to each other, like a friend to a friend; they prayed together. He watched over her while she took a brief rest. In one of her letters she writes: "Jesus has not left me all alone, he allows my Guardian Angel to remain with me always." We find this in her *Diary*, June 21, 1900: "This evening after my Confession to Father Vallini, I felt suddenly agitated and disturbed; it was a sign that the devil was near. . . . The enemy, who had been concealed for some hours, appeared in the form of a tiny little fellow, but so horrible that I was almost overcome with fear. Continuing to pray, all at once I began to experience many blows on my shoulder and this lasted for nearly half an hour. Then my Guardian Angel came and asked me what was the matter; I begged him to stay with me all night, and he said: 'But I must sleep.' 'No,' I replied, 'the Angels of Jesus do not sleep!' 'Nevertheless,' he rejoined, smiling, 'I ought to rest. Where shall you put me?' I begged him to remain near me. I went to bed; after that he seemed to spread his wings and come over my head. In the morning he was still there." When she made this entry in her *Diary*—as commanded by her Director—Saint Gemma was twenty-two years old, not a child. Innocent, artless and ingenuous as a child, yet she had a very keen understanding. She believed that every Christian sees the Guardian Angel, as she herself did, and she was so surprised when they told her that it was not so.

Quoting again from her *Diary*, July 23, 1900: "What horrible temptations those were! All temptations displease me but those against holy purity make me most wretched. Afterwards he [the devil] left me in peace and the Guardian Angel came and assured me that I had not committed anything wrong. I complained somewhat [to the Angel], because at such times I wished to have his assistance, and he said that whether I saw him or not, he would be always above my head; even yesterday he promised that in the evening Jesus would come to see me."

In order that no word be lost of his spiritual instructions to Saint Gemma, the Angel requested her, one day, to write down under his dictation some basic norms and rules for her conduct. Among other things, the Angel told her, "Remember, daughter, that he who really loves Jesus, talks little and bears everything. I command you in Jesus' name never to express your opinion if you are not requested to do so. . . . When you have committed a fault, accuse yourself immediately, without waiting for people to ask you to do so. Finally remember to watch over your eyes, and think that the eyes that have been mortified shall see the glories of heaven."[9]

When necessary, Gemma's Angel could be very severe and hard with her. In one of her letters to her spiritual director she writes: "My Angel is a little severe, but I am glad of it. In the last few days he was arguing and finding fault with me up to three or four times a day."[10] At times he seems to have been really too severe with her. Once she reported, "As I was eating, yesterday, I lifted up my eyes and I saw my Guardian Angel, who looked at me with such a severe expression as to frighten me. He did not say anything. Later on when I went to bed for a little while, O my God! he ordered me to look in his face; I looked at him, but I soon lowered my eyes. He, however, insisted and said: 'Are you not ashamed to commit faults in my presence?' He darted such severe looks at me. . . . I could do nothing else but cry. I recommended myself to God, to our Blessed Mother that they may take me away from there, because

[9] *Diary*, p. 182.
[10] *Letters*, p. 25.

I could not stand it much longer. From time to time he kept repeating to me: 'I am ashamed of you.' I was praying, too, that other people may not see him in that state, because if they did, nobody would ever come close to me any more. I suffered the whole day, and whenever I lifted up my eyes, he had always that severe look on his face. I could not recollect myself for a moment. I never had the courage to say a word to him. Last night, I could not succeed in falling asleep and I was awake till after two o'clock in the morning. Finally when I heard the clock strike three, I saw the Guardian Angel come close to me and put his hand on my forehead, saying these words: 'Sleep, bad girl!' "[11]

Ordinarily the relations between Gemma and her Angel were most cordial and harmonious. Her spiritual director tells us that he himself observed her and noticed that whenever she lifted up her eyes and saw the Angel, or listened to him, she was immediately lost to this world and assumed the same attitude and psychosomatic condition of the ecstatic state; yet, the moment she turned her eyes away from the Angel she was herself again. This, he says, happened every time, no matter how often she would turn to look or talk to her Angel.[12]

One of the most astounding features of Gemma's Guardian Angel's ministry is the fact that she often sent him on errands, ordinarily to bring oral messages or letters to her spiritual director from the city of Lucca to Rome, or to other distant places and return with the reply. Often the reply was delivered by the Guardian Angel of her Director, who was a frequent caller at Saint Gemma's place. All this is said and done as the most natural thing in this world. She writes to her Director on September 15, 1900: "Friday morning I sent a letter through your Guardian Angel. He promised to carry it to you. I hope that

---

[11] *Diary*, p. 215.
[12] Fr. Germano, *Vita di S. Gemma Galgani*, p. 209.

you have already received it. He took it himself with his own hands. You will let me know at once, won't you?" She was not indulging in mere fancy; at this time, she was twenty-two years old, and had already received the stigmata. Yet, when some one suggested that this delivery of her letter by an Angel may be the work of the devil, she became suspicious and referred the matter to her Director, who instructed her on what measures to take in order to forestall any diabolic interference in this matter. To Signora Cecilia Giannini, the foster-mother of Saint Gemma, Father Germano writes: "I have received all the letters sent by Gemma very punctually." Three days later, he wrote: "I always receive the angelic letters [those brought by the Angel] faithfully. The fact is unusual, and I confess that I do not understand it at all. I have forbidden her to ask the Angel to carry them and he brings them just the same. . . . She [Gemma] ought to ask Jesus and the Angel to reassure me with unmistakable signs that would banish every doubt, otherwise, I shall be constrained to forbid absolutely such means of correspondence." It appears that the unmistakable signs were given, because this is what Father Germano wrote later after Gemma's death: "To how many tests didn't I submit this singular phenomenon [of the Angel delivering Gemma's letters] in order to convince myself that it took place through a supernatural intervention! And yet none of my tests ever failed; and thus I was convinced again and again that in this, like in many other extraordinary things in her life, heaven was delighted in amusing itself, as it were, with this innocent and dear maiden."[13]

It was during her mystical suffering that the Guardian Angel assisted Saint Gemma most lovingly. When she received the five bleeding wounds, in her hands, feet, and side, on the night of June 8, 1899, the Angel was there to assist her: "There was pain in my hands and feet and side, and when I got up I saw they

[13] *Op. cit.*, p. 211.

were dripping blood. I covered them as best as I could and, with the help of my Angel, climbed into bed."[14]

In one of her letters to her Director, she writes: "The blessed Angel, on Thursday evening, just before I began to suffer, came again. Together we adored the majesty of God Who gave me then such a deep sorrow for my sins that I felt ashamed at finding myself in his presence; I tried to hide myself, to flee. I endured this torment for some time, but the Angel then gave me courage. . . . He [the Angel] had two beautiful crowns, one of thorns and one of lilies. He asked me which I wished. I wished to obey you, Father, and did not answer at first. Then I said, 'That of Jesus.' He raised the crown of thorns; I kissed it many times, smiling and weeping, and the Angel went away."

Not only did her own Guardian Angel assist Gemma, but other Angels came often to bless her and to pray with her. This was especially the case with the Angel of Father Germano, her Director, whom she describes as being extremely beautiful and having a brilliant star over his head. "Each evening," she writes to her Director, "when you send your Guardian Angel, he comes to bless me; and in the morning to wake me; this morning I opened my eyes, but he was not there, and I almost wept. You will send him back to me at once, won't you? Tell him that I ask pardon and I will not be disobedient again. I will not do it any more. Send him back to me. My own Angel is not so severe, rather, if I am bad, so much the more he comes around to bless me."

One evening she was requested by her aunts and sister to go to see certain entertainments. Gemma did not wish to go because she wanted to pray, but she had to obey. She wrote about this incident to her Director, adding: ". . . I know my Angel was not satisfied because he did not come with me. Do you understand? I do not wish to go again. . . . I shall give this letter to

[14] *Ibid.*, p. 64.

your Angel Guardian, who will carry it to you, so do not let anyone know that I have written it." From the last remark we understand the reason why the Lord permitted this special mail service through His Angels. Secrecy was needed to protect the mysteries of her extraordinary interior life, and this was God's way to do it.

Being almost constantly in the company of her Angel, Saint Gemma acquired so much familiarity with him that she came to consider him like one of the family, like her younger brother. Occasionally she was heard arguing with him in order to have her way, so that her Director had to remind her that she was talking to a Blessed Spirit of heaven and that she should tremble before him. "You are right, Father," said Gemma, "from now on I will talk to the Angel with respect and show him every sign of reverence and remain a hundred steps behind when I see him coming." Having received the order to act less familiarly with the Angels, she found herself in a dilemma to obey the order and not to be rude with the Angel. She writes to her Director: "Last Friday evening your blessed Angel caused me some irritation: I didn't want him around at all, but he had so many things to tell me. As soon as he came in, he said: 'God bless thee, O soul entrusted to my care! . . . Of what are you afraid?' 'Of disobeying,' I answered. 'No, it is your spiritual Father who sends me.' Then I let him talk. . . . "

We shall conclude this chapter by translating some of the ecstasies of Saint Gemma, during which she was heard talking to her Guardian Angel. Her words were taken down in writing by those present.

"I am afraid . . . Oh, why do you leave me alone at such a time?" [the devil had been urging her not to go to Confession].

"It is not true, you know, that you were here; I looked around so many times and I didn't see you at all."

"[You ask me] whether I am going to be sincere with the

Confessor? Of course, and I will tell everything."

"I know, I know what is the first thing [to tell him], it is that thing that happened yesterday."

"It is not so; that is the first thing . . . Do not confuse me now!"

"Yes, I understand well: the first is that of yesterday, talk about Father Germano. . . . Sincere and obedient? I understand it all now. Oh, yes, I am going. I paid no attention to him, but he was dressed just like yourself. Don't give him your clothes any more! Let him come dressed as a devil; otherwise I nearly believed him. . . . Does Jesus wish anything else?"[15]

"After I have been to Confession, are you coming back to tell me whether you are satisfied?"[16]

There was nothing in her conduct that ever escaped the attention of her Guardian Angel; any secret thought, any little distraction in prayer was punished immediately and severely by the Angel. At the same time the tender care the Angel took of her soul and body was admirable. He often urged her to take a little more food, because she ate so little and suffered so much. On one such occasion, August 28, 1900, (from her *Diary*), after those severe looks given her, as described before, because she had concealed some of the extraordinary manifestations to her Confessor, being ashamed to talk about herself, she wrote, after a new Confession, "as soon as I came out of the confessional he—the Angel—looked at me and smiled, with an air of satisfaction: I came back from death to life again. Later he spoke to me (I had no courage to ask him anything); he asked me how I was, because I had not been well the night before. I answered that he alone could cure me; he came closer and caressed me so much, telling me to be good. I asked him repeatedly whether he

---

[15] The devil had appeared to her disguised as a guardian angel.

[16] *Estasi, Diario, Biografia, Scritti Vari di S. Gemma Galgani.* Ectasy no. 45.

loved me as before, and whether he loved me just as much. He just answered thus: I am not ashamed of you today, but, yesterday, I was."

At times our Lord Himself punished Gemma for some little faults by depriving her of the visible company of her Guardian Angel. This happened early in the month of April, 1901. Jesus had told her that for several months she would not see her Angel. Now, on April 5, 1901, Father Germano not knowing about this prohibition, as usual, sent his own Guardian Angel to bless Gemma. She was in ecstasy when that Angel appeared to her, and this is what was heard by those present:

"Yes . . . but if my Father had known of the punishment Jesus gave me, he would not have sent you here."

"Of course, I am glad . . . But are you sure it is really my Father who sends you? because, otherwise! . . ."

"O well . . . When you go back to him, kiss his heart [the emblem of the Passion], his habit, and his hand."

"Yes, Yes, I shall do everything in order to listen to his advices . . . I shall do all I can in order to carry out what he orders me to do."

"I am going to let him know soon after . . . But Jesus? Speak to Jesus . . . Is He still not pleased with me? . . . Tell Him that I ask Him to forgive me."

"But the Jesus of my heart, where is He?"

"Yes, I feel Him! But, you have come here without saying anything to Jesus? Now prepare yourself for a nice little reprimand, because Jesus had punished me!"[17]

The Angel enters in almost every single page of Saint Gemma's *Diary;* he is mentioned frequently in her letters and in her ecstasies. Her great familiarity with the Angel can be explained only by the fact that she herself had lived like an Angel, with her heart and her desires more in heaven than here on earth.

[17] Ectasy no. 54.

Chapter XI

LITURGICAL CULT AND DEVOTIONS

A S the blessed, who constantly see the face of the Father who is in heaven, as princes of the heavenly court, as ministers and legates of God to men, the Angels are more than deserving of our veneration and devotion. They, however, are creatures like ourselves, even though of a higher nature, and as such they cannot be the object of worship and adoration, the cult reserved exclusively to God, the Supreme Being and Absolute Lord of all.

In the days of Saint Paul, a gnostic sect of Jewish Essenes preached an exaggerated doctrine about the Angels, extolling them above the "only mediator between God and man," the Son of God Jesus Christ our Lord. This accounts for the prudent reserve of Saint Paul regarding the veneration of the Angels, because just then this veneration was being extolled by a dangerous sect: "You must not allow any one to cheat you by insisting on a false humility which addresses its worship to angels. Such a man takes his stand upon false visions; his is the ill-founded confidence that comes of human speculation."[1] By extolling the Angels, this Jewish sect was actually extolling the law of Moses over the law of Christ; because, they said, the law of Moses was given by Angels. Saint Paul exposes the inconsistency of that sect when he shows how they, on the one hand, tell their disciples: "Do not touch, do not taste, do not handle," and thereby flatter their vanity by letting them appear as very scru-

[1] Col. 2:18 (Knox trans.).

pulous and unsparing of their bodies, as real philosophers of old; on the other hand he shows how all such scruples and self-denials are forgotten whenever nature asks to be gratified.[2] On other occasions Saint Paul always implies respect and veneration for the holy Angels, as when he requires that Christian women should veil their head "because of the Angels," when they assist at divine service,[3] or when he shows his gratitude to the Galatians by reminding them of the wonderful manner in which he was first received by them: "You received me as an Angel of God, even as Christ himself."[4] It is through Saint Paul that we have learned about the various Choirs of the Angels and their specific names. Their veneration is permitted and recommended. This cult, however, should never derogate from the honor of Christ our Lord, Who as God is the creator Himself of all things, including the Angels. Adoration is reserved for God alone, veneration for Angels and Saints. This is why the Angel of the Apocalypse, whom Saint John was about to adore, corrected him: "And I John, who have heard and seen these things. And after I had heard and seen, I fell down to adore before the feet of the angel, who showed me these things. And he said to me: See thou do it not, for I am thy fellow servant, and of thy brethren the prophets, and of them that keep the words of the prophecy of this book. Adore God."[5] The act of veneration of Saint John was probably directed to the Angel whom he knew to be such, but in his great admiration he was excessive, and so the Angel corrected him.

The cult of the Angels is found expressed very early in Christian tradition, in the writings of the Fathers. Saint Justin Martyr defends the Christians against the pagan accusation that by

---

[2] *Ibid.*, 22. Mention of an idolatrous cult of the Angels by some Jews is found in Clement of Alexandria, *Stromata*, VI, 5; and in Aristides, *Apol.*, 14 (Syriac text).

[3] I Cor. 11:10.   [4] Gal. 4:14.   [5] Apoc. 22:8 f.

neglecting the gods they were atheists: "Yes, we admit that we are atheists, as far as your pretended gods are concerned, but we believe in the true God. . . . With Him we venerate, we adore, we honor in spirit and truth His Son who came forth from Him . . . and the host of other good Angels who escort him and who resemble him."[6]

Exactly the same answer was given to that accusation by another Christian apologist, Athenagoras. During those very early Christian centuries, especially since the middle of the second century, two pagan philosophical systems prevailed in the Roman Empire, Stoicism and Neoplatonism. These systems developed the idea of intermediary beings between the transcending God and man. These intermediary beings were called *daimones,* or demons, who were inferior to God, but superior to man and whose duty was to serve God and to govern man. In many respects they resembled our Angels and, in fact, this is exactly what the philosopher Celsus affirmed: "The Angels who come down from heaven to confer benefits on mankind are a different race from the gods, in all probability they would be called demons by us [the pagan philosophers]."[7] In order to clarify the air of the confusion created by that false philosophy, Origen explains both the proper nature and duties of our Angels and, at the same time, makes the necessary distinction between the divine worship we pay to God alone, and the honor and veneration we pay to the Angels: "We indeed acknowledge that Angels are ministering spirits, and we say that they are sent forth to minister for them who shall be heirs of salvation, and that they ascend, bearing the supplications of men, to the purest of the heavenly places in the universe, or even to supercelestial regions purer still, and they come down from these, conveying to each one, according to his deserts, something enjoined by God to be conferred by them upon those who are to be the recipients of His

[6] *Apologia,* I, 6.   [7] Origen, *Contra Celsum,* V, 5.

benefits. . . . For every prayer and supplication and intercession is to be sent up to the Supreme God through the High Priest, who is above all the Angels, the living Word and God. . . . It is enough to secure that the holy Angels be propitious to us, and that they do all things on our behalf, that our disposition of mind towards God should imitate, as far as possible for human nature, the example of these holy Angels, who themselves imitate the example of their God."[8]

It is evident that as long as such a philosophy prevailed the cult of the Angels had to be proposed and practiced with great prudence and reserve and, at the same time, it had to be explained and defended. One of Origen's disciples, Eusebius of Caesarea, writes: "We have learned to recognize them (the Angels) and to honor them according to their rank, reserving to God alone . . . the homage of adoration."[9] The same reserve seems to have been maintained by the Fathers up to the time of Dionysius and Saint John Damascene. Saint Augustine did not seem to be quite at ease when he had to explain the honor that we must pay to our Angels, for fear that the neo-Christians, just emerging from paganism, may confuse our good Angels with the *daemones* and the *dii* of the pagan religion. It was Saint Augustine who left us an excellent formula which sums up the proper dispositions we must have towards the Angels: "We honor them out of charity not out of servitude,"[10] according to the Christian rule: We serve God and we honor and venerate His Angels and His Saints. Once the Angelology of Dionysius (especially the one that is expounded in his *Celestial Hierarchies*) found acceptance among Catholic authors of the East and the West, the cult of the Angels became firmly and universally established in the Church.

With Saint Benedict, in the West, begins a tradition of faith, love and devotion to the Holy Angels that grew steadily from

[8] *Ibid.,* IV, 5.　　　[9] *Praep. Evang.,* VII, 15.　　　[10] *De Vera Religione,* 55.

Pope Saint Gregory the Great to Saint Bernard, the chief and most eloquent exponent of the cult and devotion to the Guardian Angels. From then on there are no more fears and hesitations, reserve and restrictions in speaking of our love and devotion to the Angels, as had been often the case during the Patristic period. With Saint Bernard both the Angelic ministry and the cult of the Angels assumed that form of perfection which has remained unchanged in the Church to our own day: "God has given his angels charge over thee, to keep thee in all thy ways."[11] Preaching on these words of the psalm, Saint Bernard exclaims: "How these words should inspire you with respect, love, and confidence! With respect for the presence of your Angel, with love for his goodness, with confidence for his care of you. . . . Wherever you dwell, into whatsoever corner you retire, have great respect for your Angel. Would you dare in his presence to do that which you would not dare to do in my presence? Do you doubt his presence because you do not see him? . . . Not all that exists, nay, even not all that is corporeal and material is seen; for how much greater reason, then, do spiritual realities escape our senses, and need to be sought by the mind? If you accept those things that are of faith, they prove to you that the Angels are present with us. . . . Since God has given them orders in our regard, let us not be ungrateful to the Angels who execute them with so much charity, and assist us in our needs, which are so great. Let us be filled with devotion and gratitude towards such guardians. Let us love them as much as we can. . . . Let us love the Angels of God, my brethren, as the future joint heirs with us in heaven, and as actually our guides and protectors, appointed by God. . . . It is impossible for them to be overthrown or seduced, still less for them to seduce us, they who keep us in all our ways. They are faithful, they are prudent, they are powerful; why fear? Let us follow them, let us cling to their footsteps, and

[11] Ps. 90:11.

we shall thus abide under the protection of the God of heaven. . . . Should you foresee a grave temptation or fear a great trial, invoke your guardian, your guide, your refuge in oppression and in distress. Call on him and say, 'Lord, save us, we perish.' He does not sleep, he does not slumber. . . . O my brethren, may your Guardian Angels be your intimate friends; be unceasingly with those who, when you often think of them and devoutly pray to them, guard and console you every moment."[12]

We have a precious document of the antiquity of the veneration of the Angels, by the Christians of the fourth century, in the writings of Didymus the Blind, who was born in Alexandria in 313. He became blind when only four years old, but this did not prevent him from becoming one of the most learned men of his time. In his second book on the Trinity, having invoked the Archangels Saint Michael and Saint Gabriel, and having mentioned the myriads of Angels who escorted our Divine Savior ascending to heaven, and who will again accompany Him when He shall come to judge the living and the dead, Didymus addresses those heavenly spirits and exclaims: "We see now why churches and oratories have been erected in your name and for the honor of God, and this not only in our cities but also in private, in villages, in the homes, and in the fields. They are adorned with gold, silver, and ivory. Pilgrims . . . do not hesitate to cross the sea and to undertake a long and difficult journey, in the hope of being received more favorably by God through their [the Angels'] intercession and thus receive from Him far greater benefits."[13]

We have already mentioned, once before, the devotion of the people of Constantinople to the Archangel Michael, as mani-

---

[12] *In Ps. Qui Habitat,* Sermo XII. The Church has adopted these words of St. Bernard for the lessons of the Breviary: II Nocturn, in the east of the Guardian Angels, October 2.

[13] *De Trinitate,* II, 8.

fested in the great Shrine in his honor outside the city, and described by the church historian Sozomenus. In addition to this Shrine, fifteen other churches were dedicated to Saint Michael within the city of Constantinople and its suburbs. It seems likely that the devotion to the great Archangel passed from Constantinople to Italy and from Italy to the rest of Europe. Up to the ninth century, at least seven churches, in the city of Rome, were dedicated to the Archangel Michael, the first of which is mentioned in the *Sacramentarium Leonianum* on September 29: *"Natale basilicae Angeli in Salaria."* It was during the seventh century that the *Moles Adriana,* the present *Castel Sant' Angelo,* was transformed by the Popes into a basilica in honor of Saint Michael. The apparition of Saint Michael on Mount Gargano in Apulia was commemorated with a basilica in his honor and a feast on May 8.

It is remarkable that whatever feast in honor of the Angels is permitted by the Church, it is always in honor of one of the three Archangels, Saint Michael, Saint Gabriel, and Saint Raphael, of the Guardians Angels, or of all the Angels, but never in honor of any of the Choirs of Angels as such, as for example, in honor of the Seraphim, of the Thrones, of the Dominations, etc.

The feast of the Guardian Angels, which the Church celebrates on October 2, was formerly not distinguished from the feast of Saint Michael, which was celebrated on May 8 in the East, and on September 29 in the West. Little by little a separate day was appointed for the veneration of our Guardian Angels. This custom seems to have started in Spain through the zeal and devotion of the various Military and Religious Orders, and March 1 was the date for their Feast. A special office in honor of the Guardian Angels, composed by the Franciscan John Colombi, was first approved by Pope Leo X in a bull dated April 18, 1518. From Spain this Feast passed to other countries. Pope Clement IX, in 1667, assigned it to the first Sunday of

September, adding an octave to the office. Finally, Pope Clement X, on September 13, 1670, raised the Feast of the Guardian Angels to a higher rank and extended it to the whole Church, at the same time changing the date to October 2. However, Germany and part of Switzerland continued to observe the Feast on the old date. Leo XIII, on July 5, 1883, raised the rank of this Feast to double major, a rank which it still retains.

In addition to the Feast in honor of our Guardian Angels (the Angels of the individual person), a few places, like the old town of Valencia in Spain, honored the Guardian Angel of the city with an annual Feast and, in 1411, an office was composed in his honor. Pope Sixtus V, on February 5, 1590, allowed an office in honor of the Guardian Angel of the Kingdom of Portugal and dependencies. Such offices could be recited only by special concession of the Holy See.[14]

The names of the holy Angels were always regarded as a powerful invocation in time of need and distress. It was natural for such invocations to be repeated and multiplied in form of litanies, and thus various litanies of the Angels came into existence. We can see the beginning of such invocations in those inscriptions found engraved in marble, or in form of *graffiti*, at the major shrines of the Archangel Michael, as for example in the two following ones dating back to the fourth century: "Archangel Michael, have pity on thy city" (*Archangele Michael eleeson ten poli sou*), "Holy and terrible Archangel Michael, come to the aid of thy servant Charilaos" (*Agie kai fobere Michael archangele boethi to doulo sou Charilao*). The Gnostic sects had a superstitious practice, consisting of wearing amulets as charms against evils, inscribed with words like this one: "Michael, Gabriel, Raphael, protect the wearer (of this amulet)."

The Litanies of the Angels were rather long, enumerating and invoking all the nine Choirs. The Holy See has never en-

[14] J. Duhr, *Dictionnaire de Spiritualité,* at the article, "Anges."

couraged this form of devotion to the Angels. These litanies were forbidden with a number of others, first by Pope Clement VIII, in 1601, then by Benedict XIV. However, those decrees have been mitigated by Leo XIII, February 11, 1898, in the sense that outside of the litanies approved for public use (the litanies of the Saints, of the Blessed Virgin, of the Holy Name), other litanies approved by the local Ordinary may be used for private devotion. This means that if one of those Angels' litanies were approved by a Bishop, it may be privately used in that diocese.[15]

Confraternities and Associations

The expansion of the devotion to the Holy Angels, and the institution of new feast days in their honor saw the establishment of Confraternities[16] to promote that devotion. We find such Confraternities in Rome, in Paris and other great centers. Provincial councils have often encouraged such associations, as for example the II Plenary Council of Baltimore, in 1866, where among other suggestions and recommendations for the advancement of the Catholic life in America, we find this one: "It is also opportune to favor associations for the veneration of the Holy Angels, especially our Guardian Angels, which devotion is highly recommended to all by the Fathers of the council."[17] More or less the same decisions and recommendations are found in the councils of Reims of 1853, in Chapter XII, *De cultu*

[15] *Ibid.*, p. 615 f.

[16] By Confraternities it is understood an association of the faithful, legally erected by ecclesiastical authority for the exercise of some work of piety or charity and for the advancement of public worship. When a confraternity has the right of affiliating other confraternities to itself it is called an Archconfraternity. The classical centuries for confraternities were the fifteenth and sixteenth.

[17] *Con. Plen. Baltimorense*, II, t. X, c. III.

Angelorum; in the council of Prague of 1860; in the council of Utrecht of 1865; in the council of Colosza of 1863, where it is recommended that young school children should become accustomed to turn to their Guardian Angel in all their needs. The councils of Ravenna, in 1855, and that of Urbino, in 1859, took similar decisions.

It was during the past century that the Archconfraternity of the Archangel Saint Michael was first approved by Pope Pius IX and then formally erected by Pope Leo XIII, in 1878, with headquarters first in the church of Saint Eustace and then, the following year, in the church of S. Angelo in Pescheria in the city of Rome. A similar Archconfraternity in honor of Saint Michael was erected in France at Mont-Saint-Michel, in 1867.

A new surge of interest and devotion is taking place in our own days. A new world-wide association in honor of the Holy Angels, appropriately named *Philangeli,* has been established, with Episcopal approval, in many countries since 1950. At present the *Philangeli* association is found in England, in Canada, in America, in Australia, in India, in Rome itself. As the name implies, the members of this Association wish to become real friends of the Angels. Object of this new society which is open to all men and women, clerical, religious, and lay is to invoke the holy Angels for the conversion of the world and for the establishment of the reign of Christ the King and to pray for the mutual intention of the members of the association. Besides the feast days of the three Archangels and that of the Guardian Angels, the *Philangeli* honor our Blessed Lady under the title of Queen of Angels on August 2 (Portiuncula or Saint Mary of the Angels). The association had its beginning in England in 1950.

The real devotion to the Holy Angels should consist in imitating them. The good Angels remained loyal to God during the period of their probation in spite of the scandal and the seduction of Satan and his followers. The good Angels never sinned. They always did the will of the Father Who is in heaven. The Savior of mankind seems to have reminded us of this truth when He taught us to pray: "Thy will be done on earth as it is in heaven." To be God-centered and never to depart a moment from gazing at the Blessed Beauty of the Triune God, even while engaged as our guardians here on earth, may be perhaps something that is far beyond our present mortal condition to imitate, yet walking in the presence of God in the semi-darkness of our faith and doing His will, is something we can accomplish with God's grace. Thanking God for all His innumerable blessings bestowed on each of us, praising Him for His exceeding glory, goodness, and love is something that man can and should do in all places and at all times. Another characteristic of our good Angels is hatred of sin and of every imperfection in the service of God; innocence and the careful avoidance of sin in any form and degree will make us both dear and similar to them. Singing to God in our heart, praising and adoring His Name, living in heaven while still pilgrims on earth, above the stars while still threading our way in the dim light of here below, these are the things that our Saints, the real friends of the Angels, have done and still do. They thus became angels on earth, heavenly men and women.

In closing these few and imperfect studies about the Holy Angels, we humbly greet those heavenly spirits with the words of an old hymn in their honor:

"O living Stars of Heaven—Lilies of Paradise,"[18] lead and protect us in this life that we may be permitted to join your ranks in the next!

---

[18] "O viva coeli sidera / Et paradisi lilia / Nobile Decus Patriae / Dei gaudentes facie."

BIBLIOGRAPHY

(The Abbreviations PG and PL stand for Migne's *Patrologia Graeca* and *Patrologia Latina* respectively.)

ACTA Sanctorum. 3rd ed., Paris, 1863-69.

AQUINAS, Thomas, St. *Summa Theologica*, I., q. 50 ff.; q. 106 ff., Marietti, Turin, 1939. *Summa contra Gentiles*, II, 16 ff., Vatican edit., 1934. *Opusculum XV, De Substantiis Separatis, seu De Angelorum Natura*, Bergamo, 1741.

BERNARD, of Clairvaux, St. *Liber de Consideratione. In psalmum "Qui Inhabitat," Sermones XI-XIV. In Dedicatione Eccl., Sermo IV. Sermones in Cantica*, PL, vol. 182 ff.

BLACKMORE, Rev. Simon A. *The Angel World*. Cleveland, J. W. Winterich, 1927.

CEUPPENS, F. *De Historia Primaeva*. Rome, 1934. *Theologia Biblica*, Rome, 1938.

CHARDON, Abbe G. *Memoirs of a Seraph*. From the French. Baltimore, J. Murphy and Co., 1888. *L'Ange et le prêtre*, Paris, 1899.

DAMASCENE, John, St. *De Fide Orthodoxa*, PG, vol. 94.

DANIELOU, J.-HEIMANN, D. *The Angels and Their Mission*. Westminster, Md., The Newman Bookshop, 1957.

HEIDT, William G. O.S.B. *Angelology of the Old Testament*. Washington, The Catholic University of America Press, 1949.

HOUCK, Frederick A. *Our Friends and Foes; or the Angels, Good and Bad*. St. Louis, B. Herder Book Co., 1948.

HUSSLEIN, Joseph C., S.J. *The Spiritual World about Us*. Milwaukee, The Bruce Co., 1934.

KNABENBAUER, Iosephus. *Commentarius in Danielem Prophetam, Lamentationes et Baruch*. Paris, 1891.

LANGTON, Edward. *The Ministries of the Angelic Powers according to the Old Testament and Later Jewish Literature*. London, 1936.

LEPICIER, Alexis M., Card. *The Unseen World*, translated from the French. London, 1931.

MARY PAULA, Sr. *Presenting the Angels*. New York, Benziger Bros., 1935.

MATTEI, PASCAL de, S.J. *Devotion to the Guardian Angels*. Translated from the Italian. Baltimore, Kelly and Piet, 1866.

McASTOCKER, David P. *Speaking of Angels.* Milwaukee, The Bruce Co., 1946.

NIKEL, Johannes. *Die Lehre des Alten Testamentes über die Cherubim und Seraphim.* Breslau, 1890.

O'CONNELL, Raphael V. *The Holy Angels.* New York, P. J. Kenedy and Sons, 1923.

OEHLER, Gustav F. *Theology of Old Testament* (trans. by G. E. Day) New York, 1893.

PESCH, Christian, S.J. *Die Heiligen Schutzengel.* Freiburg, 1917.

POHLE, Joseph. *God the Author of Nature and the Supernatural.* Adapted from the German by A. Preuss. St. Louis, B. Herder Book Co., 1942.

PRAT, Fernand, S.J. *The Theology of St. Paul,* 2 Vols. Translated from the French. Westminster, Md., The Newman Bookshop, 1952.

PSEUDO-DIONYSIUS, the Areopagite. PG, Vol. III. *On the Divine Names; On the Celestial Hierarchies.* English translation from the Greek original by J. Parker. London, 1897.

SCHICK, Erich. *Die Botschaft der Engel im Neuen Testament,* 2nd edit., Basel, 1947.

SCHNEWEIS, Emil, O.F.M.Cap. *Angels and Demons according to Lactantius.* Washington, The Catholic University of America Press, 1944.

SELLIN, Ernst. *Theologie des Alten Testaments.* Leipzig, 1933.

SUAREZ, Franciscus, S.J. *Opera Omnia,* Vol II: *De Angelis.* Edit. Vives, Paris, 1856.

TROMBELLI. *Trattato degli Angeli Custodi.* Bologna, 1747.

ARTICLES

ALBRIGHT, William F. "What were the Cherubim?" *The Bibical Archeologist,* Vol. I (1938).

DAVIDSON, A. B. "Angelology." *A Dictionary of the Bible,* Vol. I (edit. Hastings).

DUHR, Joseph. "Anges." *Dictionnaire de Spiritualité,* Vol. I. Beauchesne, Paris, 1937.

GRUENTHANER, Michael, S.J. "The Scriptural Doctrine on First Creation." *The Catholic Biblical Quarterly,* Vol. IX (1947).

LAGRANGE, M. J. "L'Ange de Jahve." *Revue Biblique,* Vol. XII (1903).

McKENZIE, John L. "The Divine Sonship of the Angels." *The Catholic Biblical Quarterly,* Vol. V (1943).

STEIN, Bernard. "Der Engel des Auszugs." *Biblica,* Vol. XIX (1938).

*If you have enjoyed this book, consider making your next
selection from among the following . . .*

At your bookdealer or direct from the publisher.

Prices guaranteed through December 31, 1993.